Frontispiece.—U.S. Army T-2 Fokker, Rockwell Field, California, Oct. 5, 1922.

SMITHSONIAN ANNALS OF FLIGHT
VOLUME 1 • NUMBER 1

The First Nonstop Coast-to-Coast Flight and the Historic T-2 Airplane

Louis S. Casey
Curator of Flightcraft Division

SMITHSONIAN INSTITUTION • NATIONAL AIR MUSEUM

WASHINGTON, D.C. • 1964

Second Printing, 1966
Third Printing, 1972
Fourth Printing, 1973
Fifth Printing, 1978

For sale by the Superintendent of Documents, Government Printing Office
Washington, D.C. 20402

Stock No. 047-005-00001-9

Contents

	Page
FOREWORD	VII
PREFACE	IX

FLIGHT OF THE T-2

Introduction	1
The First Attempts	8
The Coast-to-Coast Flight	19

THE AIRPLANE

Technical Details of the T-2	35
Wings	35
Fuselage	40
Engines	46
Genealogy of the T-2	48
The Constructors	48
The Aircraft	56

APPENDIX

War Department, Air Service, Engineering Division, Contract 344–T, June 30, 1922	76
Anthony Fokker as Aircraft Designer	84
Log of Accompanying DH–4B, Rockwell Field, Calif., Nov. 3, 1922	88
BIBLIOGRAPHY	90

Foreword

The impact of man-made flight upon society has extended to all phases of our life—scientific, political, economic, social, and educational. With this influence has come a whole new science of aeronautics and astronautics.

Military science has changed almost completely. A great new transportation system and important new industries have developed. The peoples of the world are now next-door neighbors. Our educational processes reflect the new geographical, scientific, and language needs developed by these changes. This revolution has occurred in the less than sixty years between the Wright brothers first flight, on December 17, 1903, and the first orbital space flight. In this brief period the rapid pace of flight development has outrun the orderly recording and documentation of its history.

This crowded and on-going chapter of American history is the subject of a new series of publications, *Smithsonian Annals of Flight*, of which this paper is the first. By this means the National Air Museum of the Smithsonian Institution will add to the published literature of flight history and will record important aspects of that history, particularly as they relate to the collections of the Museum.

It is the hope of the Smithsonian Institution that this series will be useful to historians and research students and also to the large public that takes pride in this great and important area of American and world development.

S. DILLON RIPLEY
Secretary, Smithsonian Institution

Preface

In this first number of the *Smithsonian Annals of Flight*, Louis S. Casey, Curator and Head of the Flight Craft Division, tells of the first successful nonstop coast-to-coast flight—that of the historic T–2 airplane now in the collections of the National Air Museum. The author's narrative describes the two attempts that preceded the flight, and he provides a technical description of the T–2 well illustrated with drawings and photographs, plus a complete geneology of the plane.

In recording and developing the history of the flight, the author quotes recent letters from the pilots, Col. Oakley G. Kelly and Col. John A. Macready, concerning their experiences on the historic flight. The technical analysis of the T–2 includes detailed descriptions of the planes from which it was evolved—the D-VIII, F-II, F-III, and, finally, the F-IV that was modified into the T–2. The descriptions are supported by 11 drawings giving dimensions and construction details for each of the above-mentioned aircraft.

Also discussed is the relationship of the builder of the T–2, Anthony H. G. Fokker, and his chief constructor, Reinhold Platz, who was responsible for essential parts of its design, principally the full-cantilever wing that contributed so much to its success as an airplane.

PHILIP S. HOPKINS
Director, National Air Museum

June 30, 1964

FLIGHT OF THE T-2

Introduction

The T–2 stands in the annals of American aviation as the first airplane to make a nonstop flight from coast to coast in the United States, a flight that became recognized as the "magic measure" for evaluating new developments in air transportation. The two pilots on the flight, Lts. Oakley G. Kelly and John A. Macready, received, among the many congratulatory telegrams, one from Ezra Meeker of New York: "Congratulations on your wonderful flight, which beats my time, made seventy-one years ago [1852] by ox team, at two miles an hour, five months on the way . . . ." Comparing the five months' time mentioned in this telegram and the present-day jet transport schedules of slightly under 5 hours, the flight of the T–2 on May 2–3, 1923, in 26 hours 50 minutes still stands as an historic event.

The American continent had been spanned through the air in 1911 by Calbraith Perry Rodgers in the Wright EX "Vin Fiz." Rodgers' flight was made at a time when personal courage and resourcefulness far exceeded the technical capabilities of the machine, and, although recorded as the first flight ever to make the crossing, it was accomplished by a succession of short jumps. The longest American flight on record, in 1923, was that from Omaha, Nebr., to Philadelphia, Pa., by Capt. Eddie Rickenbacker.

Lt. Oakley G. Kelly and Lt. Muir S. Fairchild, during the winter of 1921–22, conceived the original idea for the transcontinental flight. In a letter to the author, September 30, 1959, Kelly describes how the idea was finally converted into action.

> In order to promote the idea, a large map of the United States showing the proposed route from New York to San Diego was posted on the wall in my office near the entrance to the pilots' locker room. Shortly the inevitable happened, when Col. Thurman H. Bane, Commanding Officer of McCook Field [Dayton, Ohio] at that time, came walking in to don flying clothing and paused to inquire, "What's this?" In those days a good story was necessary to secure approval of a cross-country trip of over 100 miles. Later events indicated that from that moment we were on our way except for approval from Washington, and the all important feature of finding an airplane that was capable of making the flight.

In the same letter Kelly added that the lack of a suitable plane for such a flight had served to dampen somewhat his enthusiasm and that of Lt. Fairchild.

The only airplane which might have accomplished the task was the German-built Junkers JL–6 powered by a BMW 185-hp engine. But because extensive conversion would have been necessary and because the entire equipment was of foreign design and manufacture, the U.S. Air Service passed it up without serious consideration. (World War I was only four years behind them.) However, on December 4, 1920, the Air Service had contracted with Anthony H. G. Fokker to construct two single-engine monoplanes of the F-IV design, an enlarged version of Fokker's smaller and successful commercial aircraft, the F-III. Both these planes had been designed by the little-known Reinhold Platz, Fokker's "chief constructor," who had also designed the majority of the highly rated Fokker planes including the D-VII, D-VIII, and F-II. Of the F-IV, only these two aircraft were built. Completed at the Fokker plant at Veere, Island of Walchern, Netherlands, they were placed aboard the transport *Cambria* at Antwerp, Belgium, on March 19, 1922, and arrived at the Army base in Brooklyn, N.Y., about March 30, 1922. From there they were transhipped to McCook Field at Dayton, Ohio.

After uncrating and assembling one of them, Lt. Kelly was assigned as project officer to fly the airplane for acceptance flight tests. His initial flight was made on June 1, 1922, and immediately after landing Kelly advised R. B. C. Noorduyn, Fokker's representative, that in his opinion the airplane was capable of the proposed nonstop transcontinental flight. On June 30, 1922, a contract (no. 344) was signed for purchase of the airplanes, at a price per plane of $30,000, the cost of a small, business-type airplane of today. During this same summer of 1922, Lt. Fairchild was involved in an accident while testing an early model of the reversible-pitch propeller and was forced to withdraw from the projected flight.

Lt. Ernest W. Dichman, assistant chief of the Structure and Airplane Section of Wright Field, volunteered to carry out static tests on the wing of the unassembled F-IV, still in storage, to determine the maximum load that could be carried. Subsequent to Lt. Dichman's tests, flight tests were made to determine the ceiling limitations with varying loads. These were correlated with a time and distance factor to determine the ability of the aircraft to clear the high points along the proposed route. Lt. Dichman's report was so complete that Gen. Mason M. Patrick, Chief of the Air Service, immediately approved the flight on August 10, 1922, while on one of his regular inspection trips to McCook Field. All the

Figure 1.—Lt. Kelly and Lt. Dichman standing by T-2 plane used in nonstop flight.

engineering details associated with the flight were directed by Lt. Dichman and his staff.

Once it had been decided to make the flight and permission had been secured, the preparations resolved themselves into two parts: planning the route and the preparation of the chosen airplane, the Fokker F–IV. Strong feeling continued to exist against the use of a foreign-built airplane for a project that was so highly American. To meet any public objections, the name Fokker was omitted in any mention of the plane and the designation T–2 (Air Service no. 64233, transport 2) was made official. All subsequent reference to the airplane carried this designation, and the flight was announced as an "engine test." (It was, in fact, a severe test for the U.S.-built Liberty V–12 engine.) However, the press and the Aeronautical Chamber of Commerce, on behalf of American manufacturers, were particularly vocal in their opposition; and L. W. McIntosh notified Maj. Shepler W. Fitzgerald (letter of September 8, 1922) of one individual in particular who was so outspoken that precautions were taken to insure against sabotage of the project.

The choice of the T–2 had been based on its lifting capacity and the relative ease of installing additional fuel tanks. Another feature of importance had been the 5-to-1 gliding angle of this plane (5000 feet horizontal distance for each 1000 feet of altitude). The selection of the route and the direction of flight were based on the prevailing winds at 5000 feet for the intended flight date (September and October 1922). Immediately after securing approval for the flight, Kelly and Dichman started on a survey flight (Special Orders 139, August 31, 1922) in an Air Service DeHavilland 4. They made the flight by easy stages from McCook Field, Dayton, Ohio, to Rockwell Field, San Diego, Calif., stopping enroute at Scott Field, Ill.; Post Field, Fort Sill, Okla.; and Fort Bliss, El Paso, Tex. From El Paso onward the pilots focused particular attention on the terrain in an effort to select emergency landing fields. They remained in San Diego four days, during which time they made several flights to investigate the passes in the area. It was concluded that 2800 feet above sea level was the minimum safe altitude. As a result of this flight enough data were gathered to select a definite route.

While the pilots were checking the route, the T–2 had been taken into the shops and the following modifications were made:

1. A 410-gallon fuel tank was installed between the spars of the wing center section.
2. A 185-gallon tank was installed in the fuselage cabin.
3. A 40-gallon oil tank was installed in the cabin.

Figure 2.—Extra 410-gallon gas tank later installed in wing of the T-2 plane. At left, Dvorak in charge of final assemblies at Engineering Division, A.S., Dayton, Ohio, and at right, Lt. Kelly, pilot.

4. A 10-gallon water tank was installed.
5. A booster radiator was installed.
6. An oil radiator was installed.
7. An extra set of controls was installed in the cabin.
8. All the furnishings of the cabin were removed, and celluloid was substituted for glass in the doors and windows. Also, a light sliding door was substituted for the heavy hinged doors.
9. The entire fuselage was recovered.
10. Standard Army Air Service 44- x 10-inch wheels and Goodyear tires (standard equipment for the Martin MB-2 bomber) were mounted on the plane.
11. The wing over the center section was reinforced with plywood to increase its strength.

12. A folding seat was installed in the pilot's cockpit to permit transfer of pilots in flight.
13. An overhauled engine was installed.

The two pilots finally assigned to the flight were Lts. Oakley Kelly and John A. Macready, then chief of the Flight Test Section at McCook Field. Both were experienced, competent pilots. Lt. Dichman (see fig. 1) was "in the running" as possible second pilot until early in September 1922 (noted in his letter to the Weather Bureau, September 1922). The choice of Lt. Macready (recorded in a letter September 2, 1922, from L. W. McIntosh, acting chief, Engineering Division, McCook Field, to Chief of Air Service and also in Air Service News Letter no. 30, November 1, 1922) was based on his extensive cross-country flying experience. This experience materially improved the chances for the success of the flight. Lt. Dichman, who was active in the planning and preparation, should receive much credit for the ultimate success of the venture. His engineering analysis of the aircraft (which resulted in the approval of the project), its modification, and, with Kelly, the selection of the flight route were major factors. But it would have been difficult to find two pilots better qualified for the actual flight than Lts. Kelly and Macready. The *Air Service Magazine* in June 1923 remarked that both men were highly skilled test pilots, "not a couple of cadets out on their first solo."

Lt. Oakley G. Kelly, AO10896, was born on December 3, 1891, at Geneva, Pa. An instructor at Rockwell Field from 1916 to 1919, he enlisted in the Aviation Section of the Signal Corps in June 1917. In July 1920 he was appointed second lieutenant, Air Service, U.S. Army. At the time of these preparations for the T-2 flight he was engineering test pilot of the Air Service Engineering Division, McCook Field.

Lt. John A. Macready, AO234616, was born at San Diego, Calif., on October 14, 1887, and attended school in Los Angeles and at Stanford University. He enlisted in the Army Air Service in June 1917 and served as officer in charge of flying at Brooks Field, Tex. He won second place in the Pulitzer Race at Omaha in 1921 and established the world's altitude record of 34,509 feet on September 28 of the same year. He also tested the Barling bomber, "the world's largest airplane," which weighed 42,000 pounds.

In the detailed official War Department Air Service Report 52.1/1, the advantages to be gained from the T-2 flight were enumerated:

First: From a standpoint of national defense it would illustrate the feasibility of transporting men, messages, equipment, or any other vital necessity, from one coast to the other in an incredibly short space of time.

Second: It would demonstrate the possibility of concentrating large numbers of airplanes on short notice at any desired point. With the increasing importance of the Army Air Service as a combatant arm, this feature alone might, in time of war, mean the saving of thousands of lives and several millions of dollars worth of property.

Third: It would be of incalculable assistance in the design and construction of long-distance bombing airplanes by providing reliable data on which to base future designs.

Fourth: It would be the first authoritative test on the reliability of airplane power plants for continuous running in the air over long periods of time.

Fifth: It would be a test on the pilots' physical endurance to stand the strain of 40 hours continuously in the air.

Sixth: From the commercial point of view, the successful accomplishment of a nonstop flight of almost 3,000 miles would demonstrate better than in any other way the practicability of commercial aviation.

Seventh: It would encourage reliable aircraft companies to organize aerial transport services, thus reflecting to the advantage of the nation at large.

Eighth: By giving encouragement to commercial aviation, capital will be attracted, landing fields established, and air routes planned. In time of a national emergency, such as a war, a well-organized and operating aerial transport would be one of the biggest factors for relief.

Ninth: In time of war many commercial airplanes could be converted to military purposes, thus serving as a valuable reserve or auxiliary to the Army Air Service in the first line of defense.

(This information appeared in a newspaper briefing of September 30, 1922, Headquarters, Rockwell Air Intermediate Depot, Office of Post Commander.)

In summary, the purpose of the flight was to test the new Army transport model T-2 monoplane, to test the Liberty motor and ascertain the longest time it could run in actual service, and, further, to test the endurance of the pilots. Finally, it was hoped that a successful flight would be positive proof that the airplane, for purposes of commerce as well as war, had come to stay.

The First Attempts

As originally planned, the flight was to be made from east to west because the plane with its heavy takeoff load could not make the altitudes necessary to clear the western mountains. However, the survey flight established the fact that obstructions could be surmounted at an altitude of 3000 feet, and flight plans therefore were altered to make a west-east flight.

The westward positioning flight estimates were as follows:

Distance	2070 miles
Flight time	24 hr 31 min
Average ground speed	83.7 mph
Gasoline consumed	586 gal
Approximate average hourly fuel consumption	24 gal

The engine, which had been overhauled by the McCook Field engine department (Maj. E. A. Hallett, chief of section), carried the following equipment:

Modified Zenith carburetors—venturi tube
36-mm metering jets
Mosler M-1 spark plugs
Delco 8-volt ignition with special 8-volt generator cutout and standard 8-volt regulator
Two 8-volt batteries
Sylphon gasoline pump
Standard radiator with 3-lb relief valve plus booster radiator

On September 2, 1922, Lt. Dichman asked the U.S. Weather Bureau to supply weather reports, with conditions listed in order of their importance as clear weather, west winds, and a full moon to aid navigation.

The T-2 was ferried westward in easy stages. The mechanics, Charles Dvorak and Clyde Reitz, and all the baggage made the trip from Fort Bliss to San Diego by train, as the 3000-ft altitude of the Fort Bliss airfield made a weight reduction necessary. On September 19, 1922, Kelly and

Macready left McCook Field, Dayton, Ohio, for Rockwell Field, San Diego, where they were greeted on arrival by the commanding officer, Maj. H. H. Arnold.

Minor changes, made to the airplane during the week of September 25–October 2, consisted of:

1. Making back of pilot's seat detachable
2. Installing continuous cord message conveyor
3. Installing shutters in air duct
4. Installing valve in booster radiator line to control engine temperature
5. Installing means to spray 50-50 mixture of kerosene and lubricating oil on exhaust valves.

A short test flight of 4½ hours was made on October 2, during which the pilots inspected the Temecula Canyon. On landing, the plane was conditioned, and October 4 was spent fueling it (using standard procedure to prevent condensation, with 40 gallons removed prior to takeoff). The airplane was positioned on the newly prepared runway in preparation for takeoff. The gross takeoff weight of the airplane was 10,695 pounds.

At 8:30 p.m., October 4, this telegram was received from the Weather Bureau:

GENERALLY CLEAR SKY THURSDAY NIGHT SAN DIEGO TO MISSISSIPPI RIVER AND POSSIBLY CLOUDY SKY FARTHER EAST CONSIDERABLE CLOUDINESS EAST OF APPALACHIAN MTS FRIDAY STOP MODERATE POSSIBLY FRESH WEST OR SOUTHWEST WINDS SAN DIEGO TO NEW MEXICO AND SOUTHERLY NEW MEXICO TO APPALACHIAN MTS SURFACE AND MODERATE TO FRESH SOUTHWEST ALOFT STOP EAST OF APPALACHIAN MTS WINDS WILL BE MODERATE VARIABLE AT SURFACE AND MODERATE WEST OR NORTHWEST ALOFT ON FRIDAY MITCHEL.

Final preparations were made, the pilots arrived at Rockwell Field at 5:15 a.m., Thursday, October 5, 1922, and a coin was flipped to determine who would make the takeoff. Kelly won the toss and began takeoff at 5:53 a.m. The plane slowly lifted off the ground and continued to gain altitude slowly until a left turn was necessary to avoid Point Loma. After this downwind turn the plane settled dangerously close to the ocean in spite of all Kelly's efforts to gain altitude, and two complete turns of the island were required before they were able to reach 200 feet. The first attempt was at last underway.

At Temecula Pass, 50 miles out, the altitude was only 1700 feet. The planned route was followed until the rising ground extended into the fog which enshrouded the hills. The pilots skirted the foothills for an hour trying to penetrate the fog, meanwhile hoping that it would dissipate. The hour's delay meant that the T-2 would not be beyond the mountains by nightfall. Furthermore, precious gasoline had been wasted, making completion of the flight to New York doubtful, so the pilots reluctantly returned to Rockwell Field. Instead of landing, however, they decided to stay aloft and try to set an endurance record. A note was dropped advising the ground observers of their intention. When they landed on the following day, October 6, at 5:11:30 p.m., they had succeeded in remaining aloft 35 hours, 18½ minutes. (The previous record of 26:19:35 had been established by Stinson and Bertaud, December 29, 1921.) However, the record had to remain unofficial because the required sealed barograph was not aboard (National Aeronautic Association letter January 19, 1923, B. Russell Show, executive vice chairman of the contest committee). In fact, had one been aboard it might not have lasted for the duration of the flight, since in 1923 barographs had not been required to perform for that length of time.

Kelly and Macready were enthusiastic over the performance of the plane and engine and had learned, through this grueling flight, the fuel consumption they could expect on the transcontinental flight. The log of the endurance flight showed the following:

Took off 5:53 a.m., Thursday, Oct. 5, 1922
Landed 5:11:30 p.m., Friday, Oct. 6, 1922
Elapsed time—35 hours 18 minutes 30 seconds
Total weight at takeoff—10,695 pounds
Total gasoline—697 gallons (4231 pounds)
Total oil at takeoff, Pennzoil triple extra heavy—35½ gallons
One Liberty engine—400 horsepower
Two pilots
Gasoline drained after flight—10 gallons
Oil drained after flight—18½ gallons
Gas consumed—687 gallons
Average gasoline consumption per flying hour—19.5 gallons
Oil consumed—17 gallons
Average oil consumed per flying hour—0.48 gallon
The rpm averaged from 1520 full out to 1160
First period (6 hours) the average rpm was 1440
Second period the average rpm was 1420
Third period the average rpm was 1350
Fourth period the average rpm was 1340
Fifth period the average rpm was 1260
Sixth period the average rpm was 1180

The pilots noted that owing to rough action of the carburetors it was impossible to slow down the rpm in the fourth period. After 18 hours, approximately 60 rpm were lost when either magneto switch was cut. After 21½ hours the generator was cut out for an instant and 50 rpm were lost while running on the battery at 1350 rpm.

Before the flight, precautions had been taken with the ignition system and much time had been spent selecting a smooth set of distributor heads. The distributor cam was vaselined, and the felt used in this cam was soaked in oil. Hard distributor carbons were used, with the spring tension reduced to a minimum. A light coating of vaseline was placed on the distributor track. The breaker points were set at .015 with a .013 spark gap, and the safety breaker had been removed.

General observations by the two pilots in regard to this first flight attempt were:

1. The oil pressure remained constant at 45 pounds during the entire flight.
2. The engine temperature could be well controlled and was held at approximately 175 degrees to improve carburetion.
3. No constant altitude was maintained: it varied from 500 to 4500 feet.
4. Only 3 quarts of water were required to fill the radiator on landing. The loss was due entirely to expansion.

Repairs necessary after this flight were:

1. Slight leak in core of booster radiator, and also slight leak due to cowling rubbing booster radiator.
2. Left exhaust manifold cracked on the elbow, and three lugs cracked on left long exhaust stack.
3. Right upper side of cowling cracked.
4. Both outside tire streamlining covers ripped from retaining ring around the hub.
5. Left forward celluloid window cracked and loose, and screws loosened in other windows.

Following the first (endurance) flight, a period of unfavorable weather prevented the departure for the second attempt. During this waiting period the T–2 was checked thoroughly. Several minor repairs were made, and at least one test flight of 2½ hours was undertaken. Several meteorological reconnaissance flights in DH–4B aircraft were made by Kelly and Macready. Weather reports received from Washington at 8:00 p.m. daily enabled the pilots to determine the probable weather conditions for the following day. It was ascertained that, while an average west-to-east wind

Figure 3.—Fokker T-2 coast-to-coast nonstop flight by Lt. Oakley G. Kelly and Lt. John A. Macready, accompanied by DeHavilland DH4B.

of 22.5 mph usually prevailed during October, other unfavorable weather conditions prevailed which entirely overbalanced this useful factor.

On November 2, Dean Blake, of the San Diego Weather Office, brought his maps to the pilots' quarters and pointed out the prevailing generally favorable conditions. At 9:00 p.m., the same evening, a telegram was received from the Washington office:

WEATHER CONDITIONS PROPITIOUS FOR START FRIDAY MORNING.

SATURDAY CONDITIONS WILL BE LESS FAVORABLE.

With the corroboration of these two forecasts, the decision was made to take off the following morning. A call was left for 3:30 a.m., giving the pilots approximately 3 hours of sleep. At 5:00 a.m. the pilots arrived at the field, where the airplane was ready on the line. They waited for adequate light, then took off at 5:57 a.m. with Kelly as pilot.

Takeoff weight was 10,850 pounds, 155 pounds greater than for the earlier attempt. The first part of the flight was a repeat of the previous attempt, with the plane flying a straight course, turning only enough to avoid Point Loma. In contrast to the previous attempt, the sky was clear and Temecula Pass was negotiated, as were the higher elevations near San Jacinto and those south of Banning, Calif. They flew an easterly course to Niland and on to the Colorado River. During the first hour of the flight they were accompanied by Lts. G. L. Weber and J. P. Richter, flying a DH–4B airplane (The log of this plane is given in appendix 3). Just after passing the Gila River, where they located the Southern Pacific Railway tracks, the pilots changed positions, and Kelly crawled back into the cabin. Macready, who had been steadying the aircraft with the controls in the cabin, came forward to the pilot's seat.

In the vicinity of Tucson, Ariz., the T–2 had to be maintained at its absolute ceiling in order to clear the mountains. On several occasions the pilots approached a high elevation without any assurance that the airplane would be able to lift over it, then, just as the summit was approached, the updraft from the mountainside boosted the plane up and over. For long periods they flew with only 40 to 50 feet clearance, for it was impossible to climb higher with the heavily loaded craft. The extreme turbulence and resulting manipulation of the controls proved extremely fatiguing to Macready. Therefore, after passing Deming, N. Mex., the pilots again exchanged positions. An hour's flying on the intended course indicated that the airplane would eventually fly right into the ground. Noting this, they turned southward, directing the plane's course over the Malpais, the ancient lava beds. As each gallon of fuel was consumed, the T–2 was able to rise a bit higher but they continued, skimming only a few feet above the trees. Near Tecolote, N. Mex., downdrafts caused by the "divide" forced the airplane to within 20 feet of the ground, barely missing the cactus and shrubbery. Expecting a crash momentarily, the pilots flew just above stalling speed, then turned and flew about 10 miles back down the slope in an attempt to burn off some fuel and gain altitude.

After leaving Tucumcari, N. Mex., the pilots changed places again. By this time it was dark, and Lt. Macready, who took over the controls, was forced to fly very close to the ground. Intense concentration was required to avoid hitting farmhouses. Because of poor visibility caused by weather conditions and darkness, it was difficult to follow the railroad tracks. Occasionally the bright beam of a railroad train assisted them in reorienting themselves. With thunderstorms on all sides, the discomfort increased, particularly for the pilot in the open forward cockpit. Attesting to the reported difficulties of the pilots, the newspapers of November 5 recorded that a storm and a tornado which swept the area covered by the T–2 had claimed 12 lives and injured 80.

From Pratt, Kans., a compass course was flown to Wichita and onward through the night to St. Louis, Mo. The pilots again changed positions, Kelly resuming the piloting, and shortly after passing St. Louis, they saw in the east the first light of day. At about 450 miles from San Diego a small crack in one cylinder had been noted. If this had been the only break, the flight could have continued to destination, but other jackets had evidently cracked during the course of the night. Just beyond Terre Haute, Ind., Kelly noted that the water supply was being rapidly depleted, and a check revealed several cracked cylinder jackets, making a forced landing probable. This news was passed back to Macready. A change of pilots followed and Macready examined the damage firsthand. By this time water was squirting in small streams from both sides of the engine. The damage was progressive, and at a point about 50 miles beyond Indianapolis, the engine temperature began to rise rapidly from the loss of water. The plane was turned back toward a field they had noted previously. During this time, Kelly, who was in the back, poured all available liquids into the cooling system, hoping to prolong the flight and effect a landing at the Indianapolis Speedway. On approaching the speedway, they still were at an altitude of 3000 feet, and Macready elected to try for Schoen Field, Fort Benjamin Harrison, near Indianapolis. The airplane was partially flown and partially glided to the field, where, after a circuit to position the plane, a landing was made at 7:15 a.m. (9:15 local time). As the airplane, with very low engine power, crossed the edge of the field, the throttle was pulled back and the propeller stopped—frozen tight by the engine heat. Anticipating the possibility of fire, the pilots jumped to the ground as soon as the plane stopped rolling.

From these experiences on this flight, the pilots decided to make their next attempt from east to west. The factors involved in this decision included the following:

San Diego to New York distance: 2780 miles

New York to San Diego distance: 2445 miles

Prevailing winds: west to east

High pressure usually accompanied by east wind along route: best condition for start from east coast; low pressures give high west winds but poor flying conditions

Light load by the time high elevations are reached if start is from the east coast

Engine can be throttled 1 hour after leaving New York; 12 hours full throttle are required if start is made from west coast.

For this flight the airplane was equipped with a 400-hp (Ford built) Liberty V–12 engine (Air Service no. 5142, mfg. no. 745), which developed approximately 325 hp at 1500 rpm, giving a power loading of 33.2 lb/hp. The engine was equipped with a Martin bomber propeller (Air Service drawing 047315). This engine was the one used in the endurance flight and, as a result, had 55 hours flying time prior to the start of this second attempt. The spark plugs had been changed, but otherwise the engine was unchanged.

Log of Second Flight, November 3, 1922

Place	Dist. (mi.)	Time (Pac. Std.) a.m.	Elapsed Time (hr/m)	Av. Gr. Speed (mph)	Gr. Elev. (ft)	RPM	Remarks
San Diego, Calif.	0	5:57	0	0			Takeoff, Lt. Kelly
San Diego, Calif.	0	6:10		0	13	1520	On course
Temecula, Calif.	60	6:50	0:40	90	1700	1520	
Banning, Calif.	90	7:12	1:02	90	2559	1520	Crossed at 3,100 ft
Niland, Calif.	185	8:12	2:02	92	130	1480	
Colorado River	250	8:51 9:10	2:41	96	139	1480	Changed Lt. Macready
Delos, Ariz.	325	9:40	3:30	93		1500	Flying at 2,900 ft rpm 1,520
Gila Bend, Ariz.	355	10:03	3:53			1520	Scattered clouds
Redrock, Ariz.	445	10:55	4:45	94	1864	1520	
Tucson, Ariz.	480	11:15	5:05	96	2386	1520	Discovered water leak in no. 2 cyl.
Dragoon Mts., Ariz.	540	noon 12:00			4613	1500	Approx. 400 ft clearance
Bowie, Ariz.	580	p.m. 12:25	6:15	93	3759		Strong S.W. wind
Deming, N. Mex.	685	1:35	7:20		4332	1500	Lt. Kelly pilot
Rincon, N. Mex.	735	2:35				1520	Course N.E. strong S. wind
San Andres Range	760		8:27	90	6800	1520	Narrow pass 50 ft clear
End of lava bed	810	2:55	8:45	92.6			Desert valley
Coyote, N. Mex.	850	3:20	9:10	93		1500	
Santa Rosa, Ariz.	960	4:40	10:30	92		1500	Dusk (cloudy)
Tucumcari, N. Mex.	1020	5:30	11:20	90		1480	Moonlight S. wind

Figure 4.—T-2 on endurance flight at McCook Field, Dayton, Ohio, April 16–17, 1923.

Log of Second Flight, November 3, 1922—Continued

Place	Dist. (mi.)	Time (Pac. Std.) a.m.	Elapsed Time (hr/m)	Av. Gr. Speed (mph)	Gr. Elev. (ft)	RPM	Remarks
Dalhart, Tex.	1115	6:30	12:20	90.5			Moonlight S. wind
Stratford, Tex.	1145	6:50	12:35	91			Moonlight S. wind
Guymon, Okla.	1185	7:20					Moonlight S. wind
Canadian River	1200	7:25	13:05	92			Lt. Macready pilot
Bucklin, Kans.	1305	8:50	14:40	89		1440	Ceiling 100 ft
Pratt, Kans.	1355	9:30	15:23	88.5		1460	Altitude 2600 ft
S. Newton, Kans.	1435	10:35	16:25	87.5		1460	1040 ft—16:45, 410 gal gas
		a.m.					
Ottawa, Kans.	1550	12:03	17:53	87			Lt. Kelly pilot
Missouri River	1700	2:30	20:20				
Alton, Ill.	1820	3:30	21:20				Missouri & Mississippi junction
Terre Haute, Ind.	1970	6:10	24:00	82			
Indianapolis, Ind.	2050	7:10	25:00	82			
Landing		7:15					

Kelly had flown 14:25 hr and Macready 10:50 hr, the forced landing having occurred shortly after the beginning of Macready's third shift. The log of the second flight is summarized in the following:

San Diego to Indianapolis	2060 miles
Time	25:05 hr
Ground speed (average)	82 mph
Fuel consumption (average)	23.3 gal per hr
Oil consumption (average)	0.58 gal per hr

A new engine was installed and the T–2 was flown to McCook Field, at Dayton, where it was groomed for an attempt at a series of world records. On April 16–17, 1923, Kelly and Macready again took the T–2 into the air on a flight which was timed by Otis Porter, with Orville Wright as official observer, both representing the Aero Club of America, the U.S. affiliate of the Federation Aeronautique Internationale. Figure 4 shows the plane in the air on the record flight. During this flight the following official records were established:

Official world's duration record: 36 hr 4 min 31 sec

Official world's distance record: 2516½ miles

Official world's record speeds for the following distances:

1500 km	73.00 mph
2000 "	72.50 mph
2500 "	71.98 mph
3000 "	71.95 mph
3500 "	71.15 mph
4000 "	70.79 mph

World's weight-lifting record: 10,800 lb with one 400-hp Liberty V–12 engine.

These records, though impressive, were looked upon as further tests for the main objective—a nonstop transcontinental flight. They gave encouragement for the engine performance required, and thoughts and plans again were directed to the transcontinental flight. For this flight the T–2 was powered by a Liberty V–12, high-compression (6.5–1) engine (Air Service no. 30393).

The Coast-to-Coast Flight

The third and successful attempt was made in an east-to-west direction, for the reasons already given, namely, that the burning of fuel would lighten the aircraft and make the western mountain crossing a reasonable certainty.

An interesting sidelight to the preparation for this flight was the insistence of the pilots that the fuel be supplied from California. Tests made at McCook Field indicated that the natural California fuels had an antiknock characteristic equivalent to 20 percent benzol added to the fuels refined in the East. This was an early application of what we now familiarly refer to as the octane rating of fuels.

The T-2 was flown to Roosevelt Field, Long Island, N.Y., where many other record flights have originated. Preparations continued. At Kelly's request, a qualified meteorologist was detailed to interpret the day-by-day weather data transmitted to them. By this time much publicity attended the project, since the experience gained in the previous flights seemed to augur success for the new trial. Many persons lent their talents and active support. Dr. Edward H. Bowie, of the U.S. Weather Bureau, Washington Forecast District, provided a constant flow of weather reports and advice. R. B. C. Noorduyn, U.S. representative for Fokker, Maj. E. A. Hallett, chief of the Powerplant Section at McCook Field, pilots Kelly and Macready, and many others busied themselves with the preparations. Maps were prepared and checked. Rand & McNally roadmaps were used, as aeronautical charts had not come into being.

On May 2, 1923, all was ready for the attempt. With a weather report indicating favorable conditions over the entire route, the T-2 was wheeled into position and given a final servicing. The pilots decided to delay the takeoff for two hours to assure they would reach Tucumcari, N. Mex., at dawn and so would be able to check their navigation prior to entering the mountains to the west. As related later by Col. Kelly in a letter of Oct. 17, 1960, to the author:

> May 2nd, ground run-up had been completed. Seconds later wheel blocks were removed, full engine power applied but to our embarrassment the airplane refused to move. The ground crew was then waved in to push on wheels, and

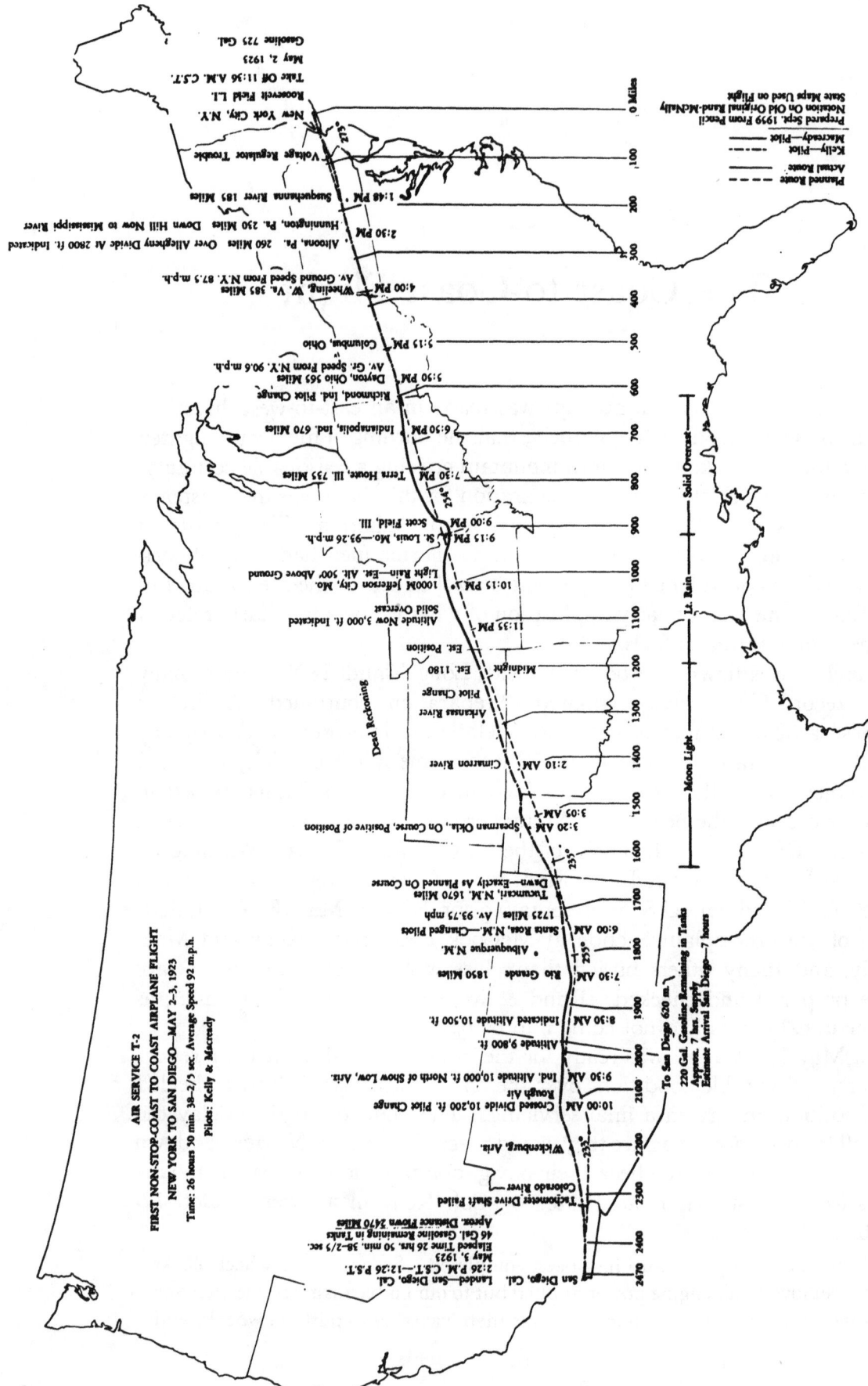

Figure 5.—Map of flight of T-2 from New York to San Diego as planned for and flown by Lt. Macready and Lt. Kelly.

with the combination of manpower and available horsepower we were able to start rolling on the dry, hard, sandy soil. There was one false start followed immediately by the official and final takeoff. The reason for the false start was due to the change in wind direction at the time of takeoff, the terrain of the available flying field, and lack of horsepower. In those days, Roosevelt Field was on the east and Hazelhurst Field directly to the west. They were separated by a ledge, or dropoff, of some 20 feet at the west end of Roosevelt Field down into Hazelhurst. Each field was approximately ¾ of a mile wide and slightly less than a mile long, thus providing a total clear takeoff distance of approximately 1¾ miles from east to west.

As the prevailing wind in the area is from west to east, the airplane was serviced for the flight in the east end of Roosevelt Field. The plan, at the time, was to take off in a westerly direction from Roosevelt, the plane being airborne before reaching the dropoff at the west end, and then have the entire length of Hazelhurst to gain altitude to clear the hangars at the west end of Hazelhurst. However, by the time of takeoff, owing to the Hudson Bay High barometric pressure, the wind had shifted to the northeast. For this reason the airplane was taxied to the ledge at the southwest corner of Roosevelt Field and the takeoff started in a northeasterly direction and as much as possible into the light breeze then blowing. As the airplane left the ground after approximately six-tenths of a mile run it was immediately apparent that we would be unable to clear electric wires and trees at the northeast corner of Roosevelt Field. For this reason the power was cut, the airplane landed with full load, taxied to the original planned location at the southeast end of Roosevelt, and immediately headed for takeoff in a west-northwest direction but with a quartering tailwind. The power loading for this takeoff was about 33 lb/hp, which may be some kind of a record even in the jet age. At least I have not heard of any jets that weigh 900 to 1000 tons.

This incident taxed not only the skill and judgment of pilot Kelly, but the structural integrity of the T-2. The airplane was loaded to a gross weight of 10,850 pounds, only 150 pounds less than the no-margin limit of 11,000 pounds gross takeoff weight. The official time for the takeoff was 11:36 a.m., c.s.t. (12:36 a.m., e.s.t.). In the *National Geographic Magazine* of July 1924, Macready gave his version of the takeoff as viewed from the rear of the airplane cabin:

> There is a row of aerial mail hangars on the far side of Hazelhurst Field.... The big monoplane bounced and bounced but did not rise. It was still on the ground when we came to the 20-foot dropoff from Roosevelt to Hazelhurst Field. I was sitting behind, watching the ground go by and the hangars getting nearer.
>
> When we came to the dropoff I wondered whether we would go over the ledge and settle down to the ground. Over we went and settled down, but not quite to the earth....

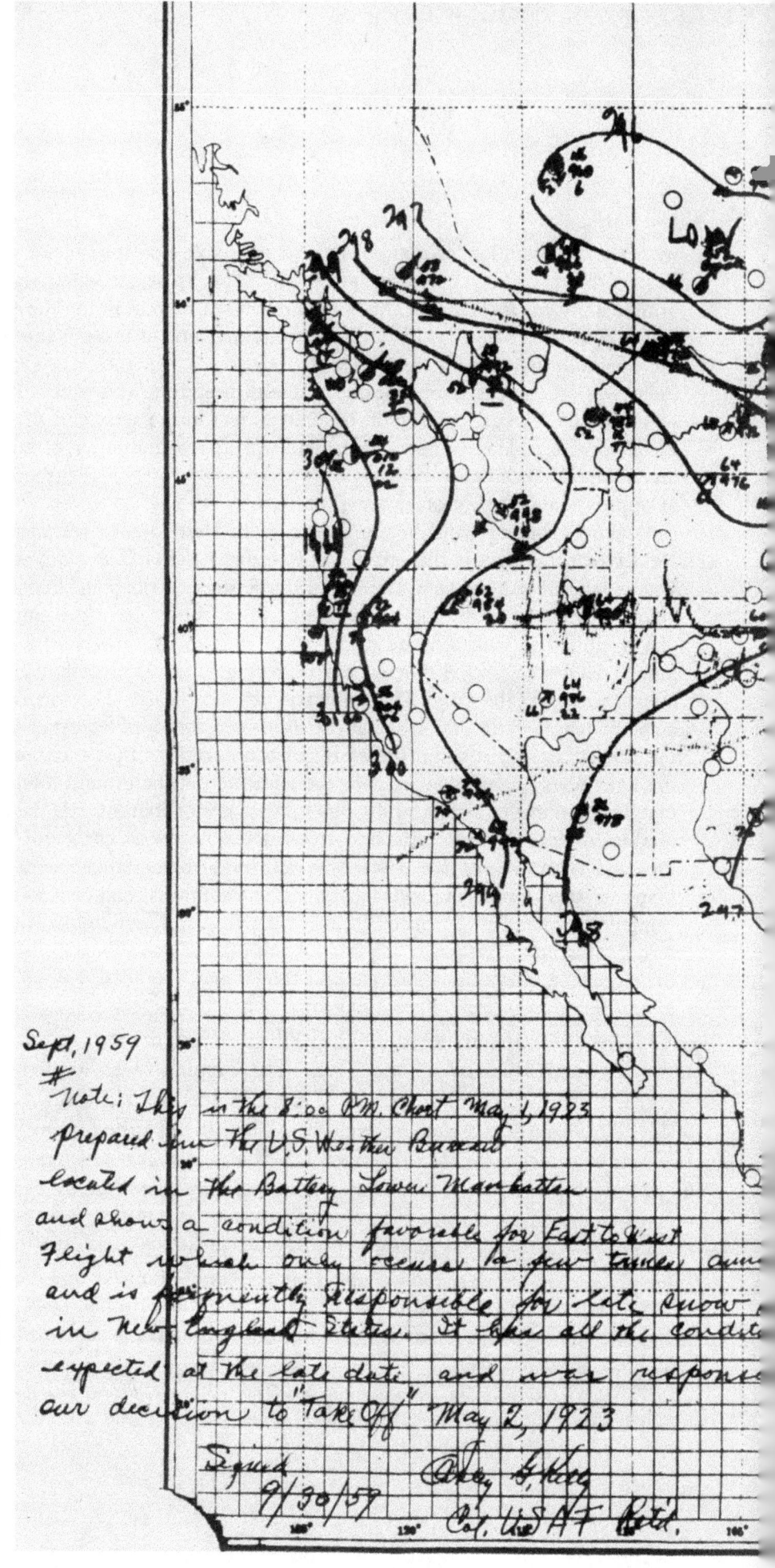

Figure 6.—Weather map for 8 p.m., May 1, 1923. On the basis of this information was made the decision to take off on the next day.

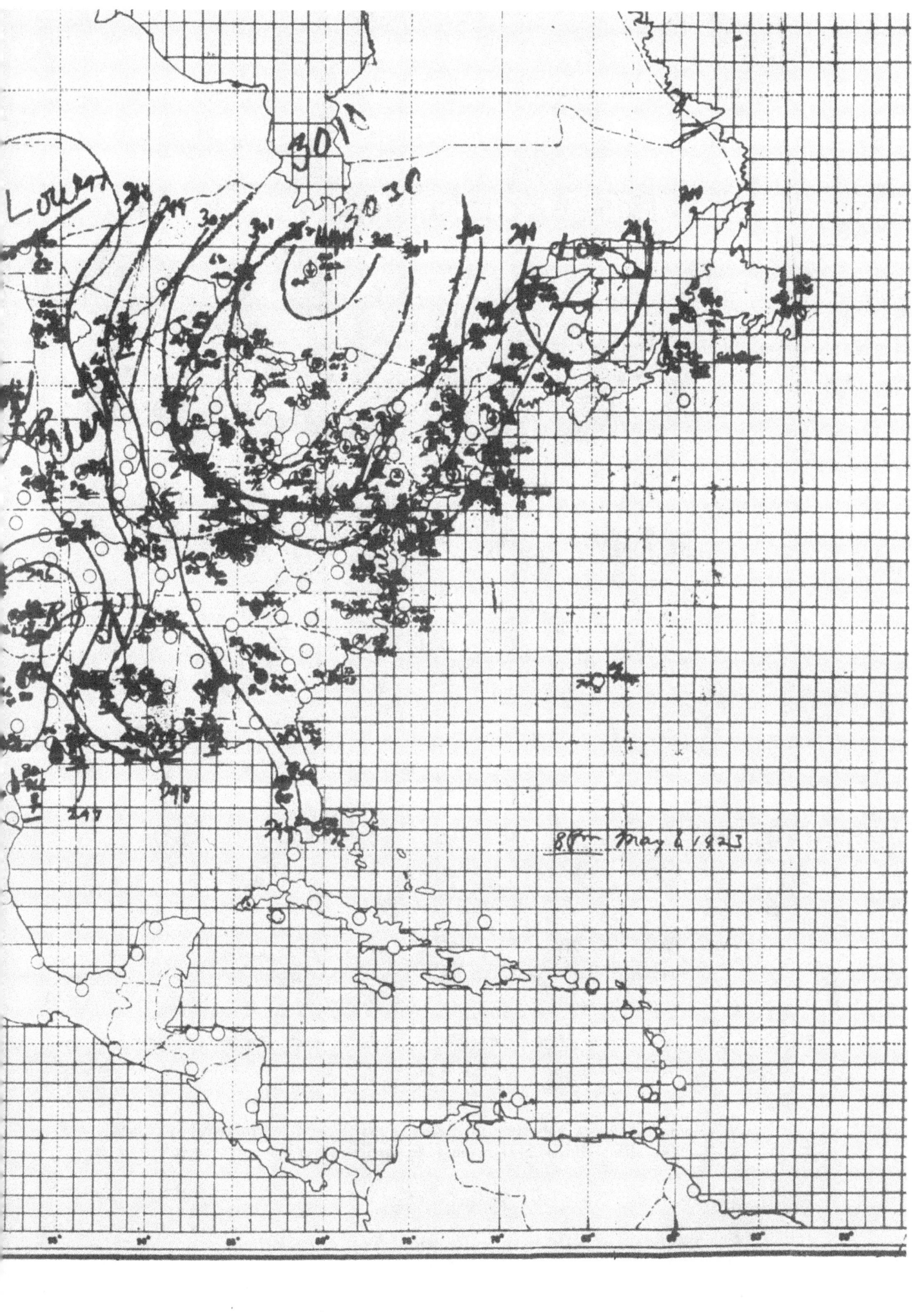

Figure 7.—Pennzoil poster.

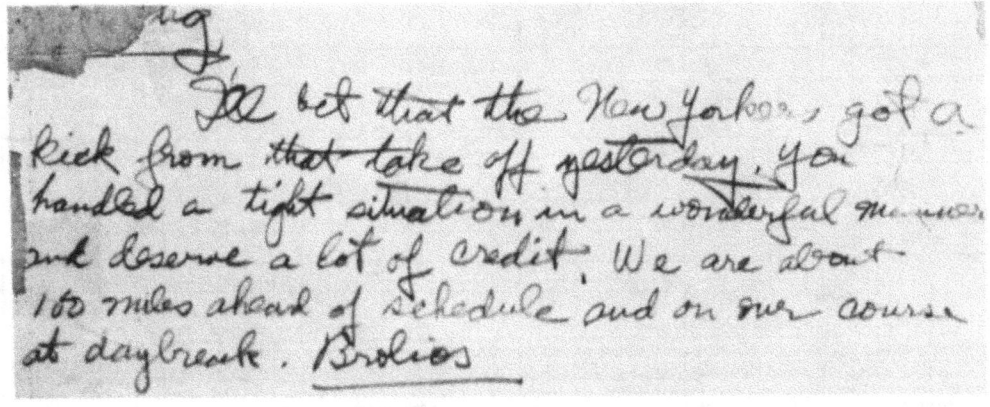

Figure 8.—Pencil note from Macready in rear to Kelly in front seat as passed over beltlike string-and-clothespin message carrier, sometime after takeoff from New York.

I would like to land the plane at the end so will continue on through if the shift is not too long or if it stretches out will change again.

Figure 9.—Pencil note from Macready, pilot, probably over western New Mexico. Later Macready decided the flight was going to be too long, as he asked for a shift of pilots at 10:00 a.m., May 3, 1923, after crossing over the Mogollon Plateau in Arizona.

The heavily loaded plane could hardly maintain itself in level flight. For 20 minutes over Long Island our climb was hardly appreciable. In fact, for the first few miles we barely cleared the poles and wires.

It appeared to me, riding behind, that we would hit the open fields, would settle down into them . . . and would barely clear the surrounding obstructions. . . . We could not talk things over until after we landed. [Three notes were passed to Kelly enroute.] At San Diego, however, I said to the wild Irishman, "Kelly, did you get much of a kick when we were settling down into those small open fields on Long Island?" "Not a great deal," he replied, "I was nosing her down a bit to get some more speed to pull us over those telephone poles."

I think you should go South west now over that ridge on the left and the high altitude will be over

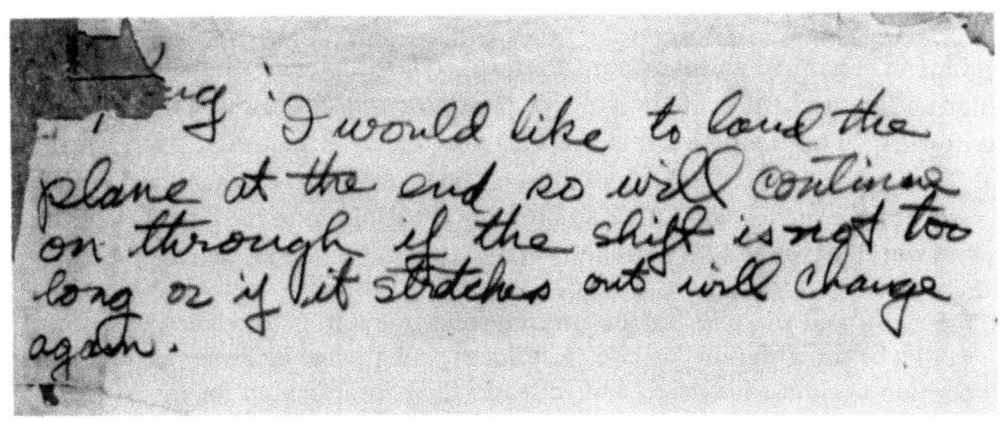

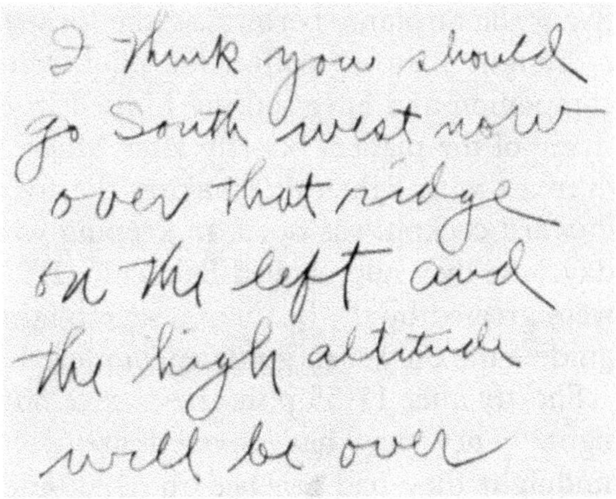

Figure 10.—Pencil note from Kelly to Macready, pilot, at about 10,200 feet in rough air, flying west or slightly north of west along the north rim of the Mogollon Plateau generally in the direction of Prescott, Arizona.

One mechanical failure soon after takeoff threatened the success of the flight. The indicator of the voltage regulator registered discharge from the batteries. The details of this are best related by Macready:

> The little things are sometimes the most important and can cause the greatest amount of trouble. About a half hour after leaving Long Island, Kelly shook the wheel for me to take the controls.
>
> It is difficult to fly from behind. There is no visibility straight ahead or to the right, and the pilot sits in an unnatural position. I thought the change would be for a minute or two, just long enough for Kelly to change his position or adjust his maps, but instead I flew from behind for more than a half hour.
>
> I was getting a bit provoked, to be left with the responsibility of keeping our course in this uneven country under the adverse personal flying conditions, and thought that my partner should not have shifted this very difficult position on me, but during this period Kelly was doing a very creditable thing, the importance of which cannot be overestimated.
>
> The ignition voltage regulator had been registering "discharge," which meant that we were flying entirely on our batteries, and we would use up these batteries in a very few hours, making a landing necessary and causing failure of the trip. Kelly took off this voltage regulator in flight, a very delicate operation, even on the ground, and adjusted the breaker points within the mechanism, so that it registered "charge" instead of "discharge," and replaced the part again.

Kelly flew as pilot until they reached Richmond, Ind., at about 6:00 p.m., when each pilot in turn struggled through the small triangular opening in the structure behind the forward pilot seat. This rotation called for considerable physical dexterity, since the back of the forward seat had to be folded forward in order to reveal the opening; and then came the problem of slithering through the opening. During the change, the rear pilot was flying the airplane, permitting the forward pilot to crawl back. Following a draught of strong coffee, the pilot from the rear retraced the path of his companion and after settling himself in the forward cockpit took over the flying of the plane. Shortly after Macready took over they entered a solid overcast with light rain, making the flying quite uncomfortable, since the forward cockpit was open, in keeping with the design requirements of that day. As they approached Belleville, Ill., and Scott Field at 9:00 p.m. they were greeted by the beam of a searchlight, which was directed upward as a guide—the only such guide encountered during the flight.

Shortly after 11:35 p.m. they broke out of the overcast into bright moonlight. They now had covered about 1180 miles along their route. At midnight they had reached the 1200-mile point and again changed pilot

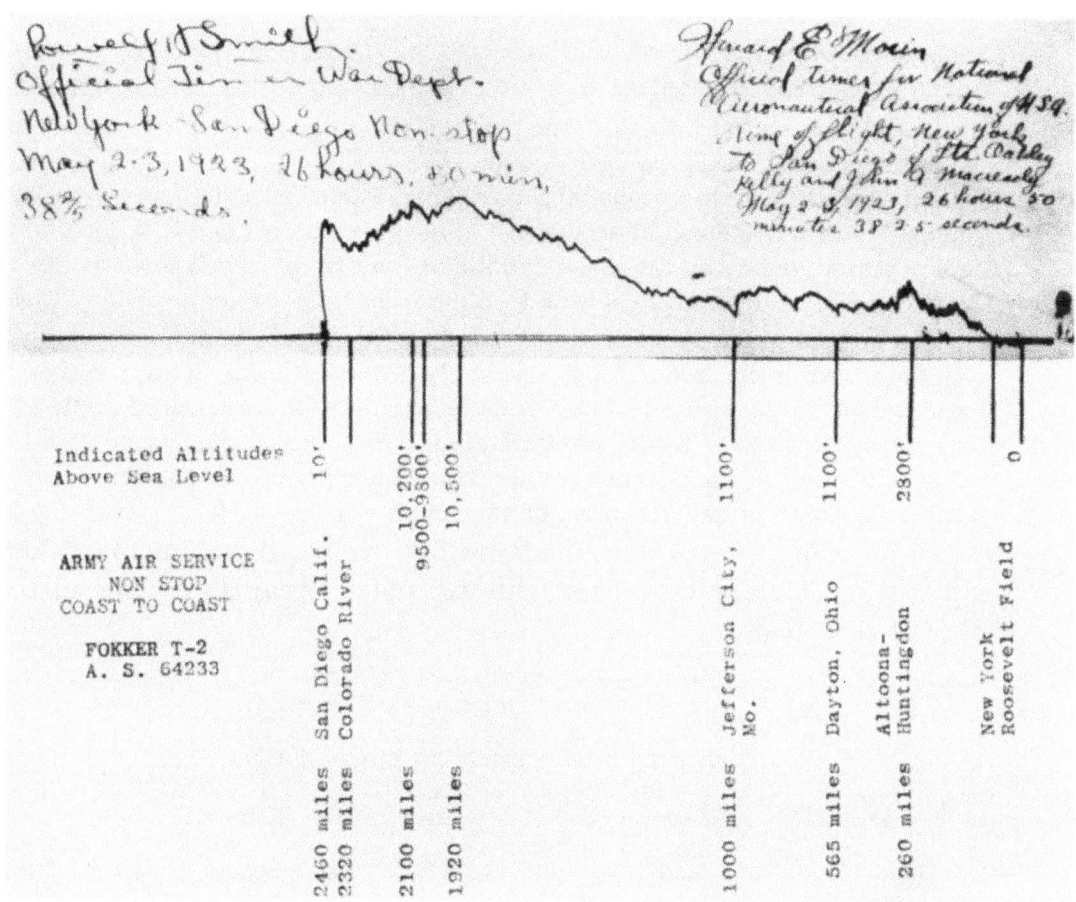

Figure 11.—Barograph recording of flight altitudes during the coast-to-coast flight.

positions. With Kelly flying they proceeded by dead reckoning until they reached Spearman, Tex. This gave them a positive check on their position and indicated that they were on course. At 6:00 a.m. on May 3 they were over Santa Rosa, N. Mex., 1725 miles from takeoff, and had averaged 93.75 mph. At this point they changed pilots again, with Macready moving to the front cockpit. When they passed over the Rio Grande at 7:30 and were 1850 miles along the course they had 220 gallons of fuel remaining, enough for an additional 9 hours of flying. San Diego lay 620 miles ahead of them, approximately 7 hours' flying time at their established ground speed.

At 10:00 a.m. they crossed the Divide flying at 10,200 feet, the highest point along the route. While at this elevation in turbulent air, they again changed pilots. In order that Macready could make the landing, another pilot change was effected as they neared San Diego. Macready related:

During the second trip . . . we passed through parts of seven states at night and were in darkness for 13½ hours.

On both these transcontinental flights we encountered storms and rain at night. This was the condition that we most dreaded. No one had flown at night across country under storm conditions, and we did not know whether a pilot could handle the unknown difficulties which might arise.

The general public marvels at our speed in crossing the continent without landing, and at the fact of being able to fly in the darkness, in bad weather, and for such a long period of time without rest; but the experienced pilots of the Army Air Service give us most credit for flying through those long nights and coming out of the darkness in the morning directly on our course. Kelly and I take most pride in that feat of navigation.

The following is an extract made by Col. Kelly from his personal log, supplied in a letter to the author with explanatory remarks by him of the coast-to-coast flight:

Log of Third Flight, May 2–3, 1923

(Extracted from personal log of Col. Kelly)

Place	Time	Miles	Altitude	Remarks
	a.m.			
Roosevelt Field, Long Island, N.Y.	11:36	00		Takeoff for San Diego, Calif. Remember clocks were not set to New York time—All time c.s.t.
	p.m.			
Susquehanna River	1:48	185		Ground speed 84 mph
Huntingdon, Pa.	2:30	240	2800	Nearing Continental Divide
Altoona		260	2800	Down hill now to Miss. Riv.
Wheeling, W. Va.	4:00	385		Avg. ground speed 87 mph
Columbus, Ohio	5:15	500		
Dayton	5:50	565	1000	Avg. ground speed 90.6 mph
Indianapolis, Ind.	6:50	670		Overcast—Macready pilot at Richmond.
Terre Haute	7:30	735		
Scott Field, Ill.	9:00	800		Avg. ground speed 93.6 mph
Jefferson City, Mo.	10:15	1000		Lt. rain, fly low, speed 93.9 mph
Estimated position	11:35	1180		Moonlight—Kelly pilot at midnight.

From St. Louis, Mo., to Jefferson City, Mo., we had followed the general direction of the Missouri River as light reflected from the muddy water was of considerable assistance as a fix or point of balance in navigating the airplane at night in poor visibility and light rain. As the Missouri swings to the northwest at Jefferson City it was necessary to take up a compass course striking cross country at about 245 degrees. Check points are scarce and all towns look alike in western Missouri and southeastern Kansas at night. By dead reckoning we checked the Arkansas River and the Cimarron later as they were crossed, but our drift to north or south of the course was not known until 3:20 a.m. as we passed Spearman, Hansford County, Tex. At this point we were 1510 miles from New York and 510 miles from Jefferson City with an average speed of 96.48 mph from New York and 102 mph on the leg from Jefferson City. Picking weather with high and low pressure areas in desired geographic sections of the continent is now paying good dividends with favorable tail winds.

Place	Time a.m.	Miles	Altitude and Remarks
Spearman, Tex.	3:20	1510	On course—positive of position
Tucumcari, N. Mex.	Dawn	1670	Position exactly as planned
Santa Rosa, N. Mex.	6:00	1725	Avg. speed N.Y. to Santa Rosa 93.75 mph
Sabine, N. Mex.	7:30	1850	Crossing Rio Grande River, 220 gal. gasoline—approx. 9 hr supply—E.T.A. San Diego 7 hr
	8:30		Altitude above sea level, 10,500 ft
Show Low, Ariz.	9:30	2035	Altitude above sea level, 10,000 ft
	10:00	2080	Over Continental Divide 10,200 ft Macready pilot from Santa Rosa, N. Mex. Changed here, Kelly now pilot.
Wickenburg, Ariz.		2210	Position checked on map
Colorado River		2320	
San Diego, Calif.	p.m. 2:26	2470	As prearranged, changed pilots to give Macready honor of landing.

Time: Left New York 12:36 e.s.t. Landed San Diego, Calif. 12:26:38⅗ sec. P.s.t. May 2 and 3, 1923. Elapsed time: 26 hr, 50 min 38⅗ sec. Average ground speed for 2470 miles 92.05 mph.

Of the end of the flight, Macready had this to say:

I wonder why we did not get more of a "kick" from our first sight of San Diego. It did give me a very pleasant feeling, to think that the terrific strain and hard work would soon be over, but I was not particularly excited about it . . . . As we wished to reach Rockwell Field and land in less than 27 hours, we contemplated no flourishes over the city of San Diego.

Diving down from 8000 feet with power on, we reached San Diego, cocked the T–2 up on the wing to swing down the main street, and passed about 100 feet above the tops of the buildings . . . . We wasted no time. The Army Air Service transport made one turn of North Island, to head into the wind, and landed exactly 26 hours and 50 minutes elapsed time from Long Island New York.

Every one was excited but Kelly and myself. We had been working in grease and dirt, without rest, for such a long time previous to the flight that

Figure 12.—Kelly and Macready welcomed by Col. H. H. Arnold, Rockwell Field, San Diego, May 3, 1923.

we had not had opportunity to think about it from the standpoint of an accomplished act . . .

Honor is its own reward. There is plenty of glory in connection with flights of this nature, and considerable satisfaction in doing one's duty as a soldier and accomplishing a feat considered by many to be impossible, but after the glamour wears off, one wonders whether the health and vitality which have been so severely taxed are not of more value than the glory gained.

The coffee and broth in our thermos bottles, filled in New York [by Mrs. Weaver, wife of the Commanding Officer of Mitchel Field] the previous afternoon, were still hot.

At least two persons had a "financial" interest in the flight. Col. Franklin R. Kenney, former executive officer of the Air Service, was among those present at the time of takeoff and immediately made a $5,000 bet with a disbelieving companion. With the successful completion of the flight he wired Col. L. H. Drenan of the Air Service: "I win five thousand dollars if Macready and Kelly are successful in nonstop flight stop will you wire my expense Macready and Kelly asking them if they will accept the five thousand as a gift to celebrate with their wives the greatest achievement in our aviation history stop you explain to them and make the gallant young bull pups take money reply Plaza Hotel. Franklin R. Kenney."

In response to this General Patrick sent the following telegram: "Colonel Franklin R. Kenney former executive Air Service wins five thousand on your flight all of which he tenders to you with his compliments wire acceptance immediately Plaza Hotel, New York. Patrick."

Macready, retelling the incident, said "One [telegram] was handed to me separately, which I at first read as a joke, but when told that it was authentic, reread." Thereupon the pilots prepared the following reply:

> To do anything that needs doing is a soldier's plain duty but when that accomplishment brings victory to a friend it makes a pleasure. With the grateful acceptance of your magnificent gift there is satisfaction in the knowledge that it pays to bet on the Army A.S.

Many telegrams of congratulations were received including those from President Harding, General Patrick of the Air Service, John W. Weeks, Secretary of War, and many other prominent persons. A particularly prophetic message was received from Anthony Fokker: "Heartiest congratulations on your great feat. Your flight is a milestone in the development of commercial aviation period in ten years the route you flew will be covered by aerial passengers and freight service just as Bleriot's route across the English channel is today."

After the flight many honors were conferred upon the pilots. They were awarded the Distinguished Flying Cross, the citations reading:

> Lieut. Kelly with First Lieut. Macready, departed from Mitchel Field,* Long Island, N.Y., at 12:36 p.m. May 2, 1923, in the Army Transport Airplane T-2, on a nonstop transcontinental flight. They encountered practically every hazard of flying and displayed remarkable ingenuity, skill, and perseverance in overcoming the many handicaps imposed upon them by the elements and the mechanical equipment used by them. They arrived at Rockwell Field, Coronado, California, at 12:26 p.m. May 3, 1923, thus success-

---

*The pilots actually departed from Roosevelt Field, Long Island, N.Y.

fully completing the first transcontinental nonstop flight in the history of aviation.

The pilots, were in addition, the recipients of the Mackay Trophy for the year 1923.

Following a short stay in California, during which maintenance work was accomplished on the airplane, and Lt. Macready found time to be married, the airplane was flown eastward, with a stopoff at McCook Field en route to Washington, D.C., where it was exhibited at the Shrine Convention. Following this exhibit the airplane was placed permanently in the Aeronautical Collections (now the National Air Museum) of the Smithsonian Institution, where it is prized as one of the outstanding in the history of U.S. aviation. Thus ends the saga of the T-2, on the first nonstop transcontinental flight.

THE AIRPLANE

Technical Details of the T–2

In the course of study and research on the T–2 itself, many specifications were found to be contradictory. The following account is an attempt to establish the accurate details, determined from the specimen itself, as it stands in the National Air Museum of the Smithsonian Institution.

Two outstanding features of this aircraft type, the Fokker F-IV, are the full-cantilever wing and the steel-tube fuselage. Since the evolution of this design is being traced later (see page 46), only the technical details of this particular airplane are recorded here.

SUMMARY OF SPECIFICATIONS OF THE T–2

Total span less ailerons	896¼ in.
Aileron overhang	29 in.
Overall span including ailerons	954 in.
Width of center section (wing)	74 in.
Length of chord at center section	179 in.
Length of chord at wing tip	117 in.
Area of aileron beyond wing tip	6.4 sq ft
Area of wing	961.6 sq ft
Weight of wing	2075 lb
Height	11 ft. 10 in.

Incidence 0° at the root—2° 15′ at the wing tip
Propeller (Martin Bomber type) Air Service drawing 047315
Engine—Liberty V–12, 423 hp at 1700 rpm
    First attempt (converted to endurance): Engine AS 5142
    Second attempt (cross-country to Indianapolis): Engine AS 5142
    Endurance flights: Engine (high compression 6.5–1) AS 30393
    Museum specimen: Engine AS A68062 (Buick built; mfg. no. B607)

Wings

Two box spars extend from wing tip to wing tip, tapering from center to tip in plan and depth. These spars form the main support structure for the entire wing and they are parallel, with 71-inch (1.8 meter) spacing

Figure 13.—Detail of front spar during assembly at Fokker factory.

between center lines. The top surface of the spars forms a continuous horizontal line from tip to tip. The upper and lower flanges of the spars are made of Danzig pine; the webs are of 9-ply (¼-inch) Russian-birch plywood with surface grain perpendicular to the longitudinal axis of the spar. The front spar at the root measures 28 inches in depth by $4\frac{7}{16}$ inches wide.

Figure 14.—Size of wing ribs compared at Fokker factory.

The rear spar at the root is 20¾ inches depth by 4¼ wide. The ribs, made of Russian birch, vary from 0.034 to 0.043 inch in thickness and are reinforced by stiffeners of triangular cross section glued to the faces of the ribs. To these ribs are fastened cap strips of ¼-inch square pine stock. The plywood covering is of rotary-cut 3-ply Russian birch approximately 1.5 mm (0.056 inch) thick. Owing to this thin covering, wood strips were glued to it on the inside surface between the ribs. Rib spacing is 17⅛–

Figure 15.—Assembled wing, showing rib spacing and reinforcement.

17¼ inches. The chord of the wing tapers from 14 feet 11 inches at the center to 9 feet 9 inches at the tip. The box construction of the wing, together with the rigid plywood skin which is glued and nailed to the internal structure, makes drag-trussing unnecessary. The rear portion of the wing, aft of the rear spar, is built up as a separate unit and is attached to the top and bottom of the rear spar by brass screws. The ailerons are supported from this rear section, and are of typical Fokker elephant-ear, or balanced type, in plan view, measuring 10 feet 11¼ inches at the hinge line and having varying chord. The ailerons, of welded tube construction, are covered with fabric and have a total area of 38 square feet.

The wing weighed 2075 pounds during McCook Field tests and had a calculated area of 961.6 square feet. The main wing structure span is 74 feet 10 inches, and the overall span including ailerons is 79 feet 6 inches. The entire structure is built up of glued wood units with brass brads used

Figure 16.—Completed wing with plywood covering installed. Platz, the designer, revealed that the wings of the "F" series of monoplanes were, in fact, geometric enlargements of the D-VIII wing.

to insure proper adhesion of the glued joints. The wing is secured to the upper fuselage longerons by four fittings and four bolts. The fixed angle of incidence is 0° at the center and −2° 15′ at the tips.

Modification of the wing for the coast-to-coast flight was required, as stress analysis indicated the weakest point to be the center section, at which point was suspended the entire weight of the fuselage complete with the 185-gallon fuel tank. To strengthen this area adequately and also to accommodate the extra 410-gallon fuel tank in the wing center section, a ⅞-inch plywood facing plate was installed on the inner face of the front and rear spars, using hide glue and screws, between the attachment fittings. The compression ribs in the center section were reinforced in a similar manner, and special bedding brackets were constructed and installed for the center section fuel tank. The wing was then recovered and given a protective coat of Valspar varnish.

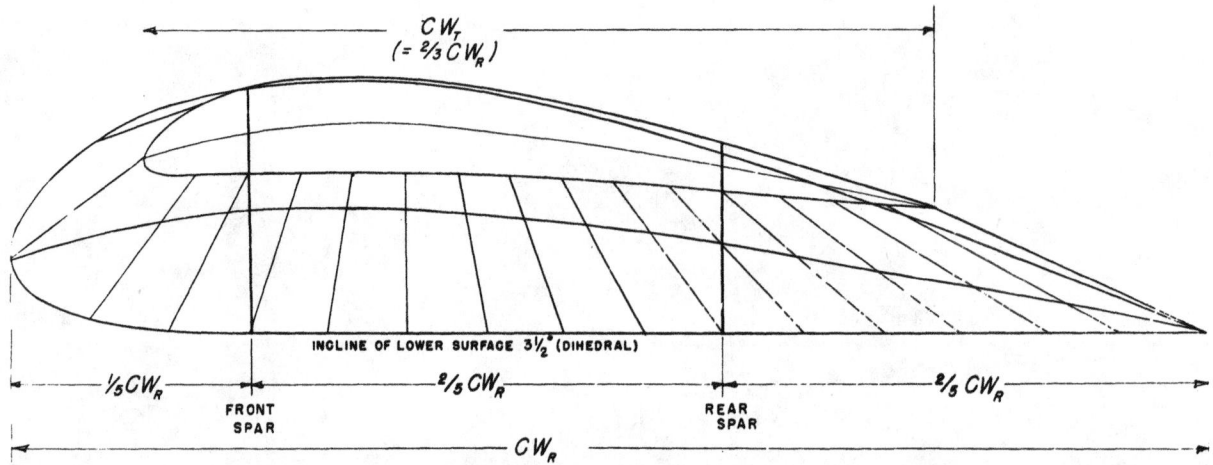

Figure 17.—Diagram of the root and outer rib of the F-IV, 1:10, Fokker T-2, A.S. 64233. The outstepped angle of profile stringers for all ribs is 3½ (dihedral). The lower edge of the root rib from the front spar to the rear spar is 0 straight 0°. The chord of the outer rib is ⅔ that of the root rib. The front spar upper edge is horizontal over the entire span. The spars run in equal (parallel) spacing (1.8 m) through the whole wing. The unsupported length of the outer wing panel is about 11.5 m. The area over the fuselage is nearly 1.8 m. The whole span without the aelerons is 24.7 m. CW_R—rib depth (chord) of the root rib; CW_T—rib depth (chord of the outer rib. This was originally sketched by Reinhold Platz, August 2, 1959, and drawn here by L. S. Casey.

Reinhold Platz, chief constructor for Fokker, in a letter to the author (August 3, 1959) provided the sketch from which figure 17 was drawn to illustrate the design and proportion of the wing.

The German order (specifications) Case A required a safety factor of 5. Calculations for the front spar showed it capable of sustaining four times the calculated load (safety factor of 4), rear spar three times the safety limit, and the front spar from the top (shear load) three times that of the rear spar from the top, and twice the safety requirements.

Fuselage

The fuselage is constructed of steel tubing longerons with an outside diameter of 37 mm at the forward fuselage and tapering to 25 mm at the rear. Cross bracing and vertical bracing tubes are welded in place at stations 1.25 m, 2.10 m, 3.0 m, 3.76 m, 4.46 m, 5.57 m, 6.66 m, 7.71 m, 8.76 m, 9.80 m, 10.80 m, 11.80 m, 12.77 m, 13.50—13.60 m, 13.72 m, using the forward cowl primary structure as datum line. Diagonal bracings in each bay are of single-strand piano wire 2 mm in diameter. Adjustment of

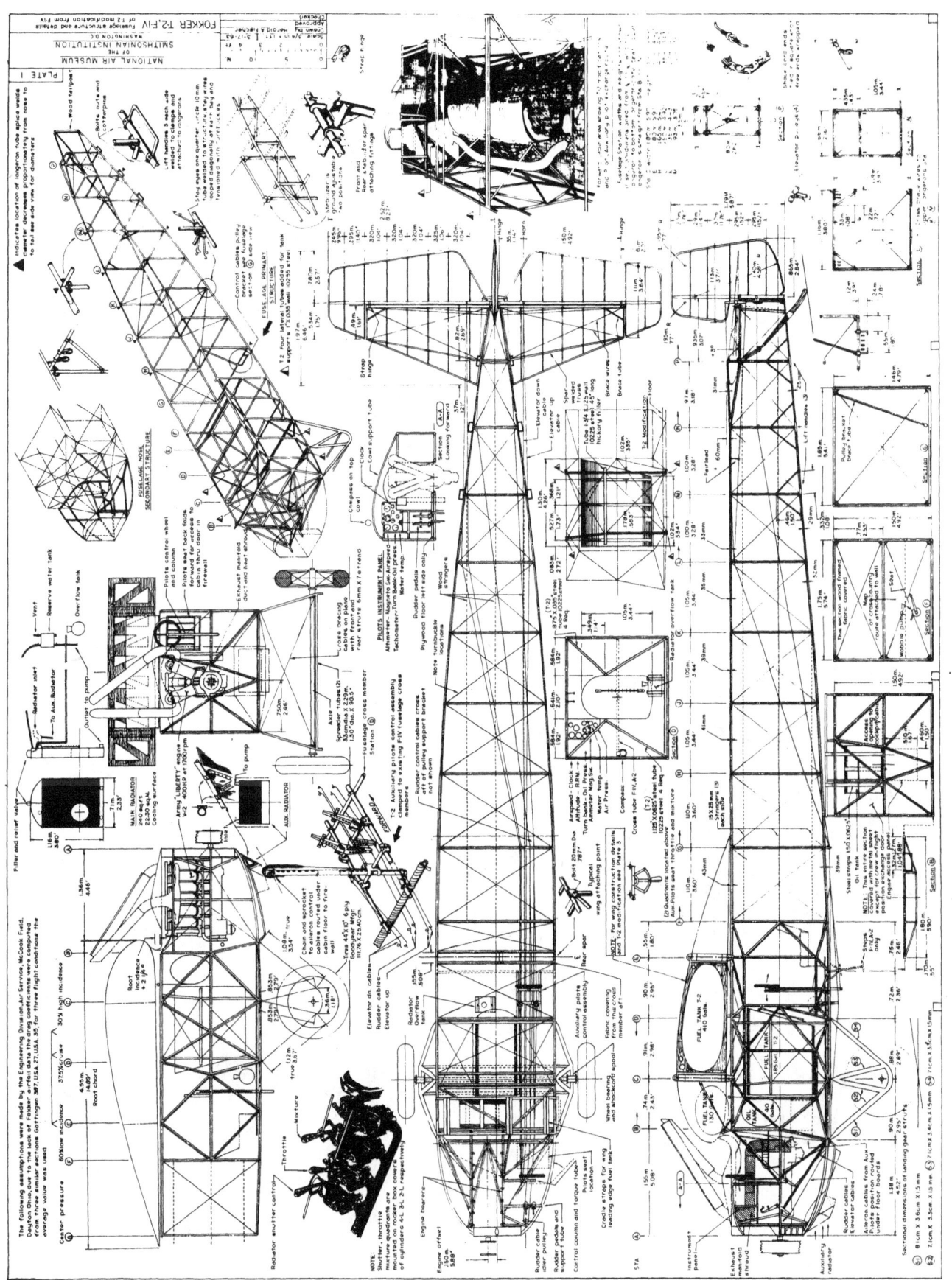

Figure 21.—Fokker T-2 F-IV, fuselage structure and modifications of T-2 from F-IV.

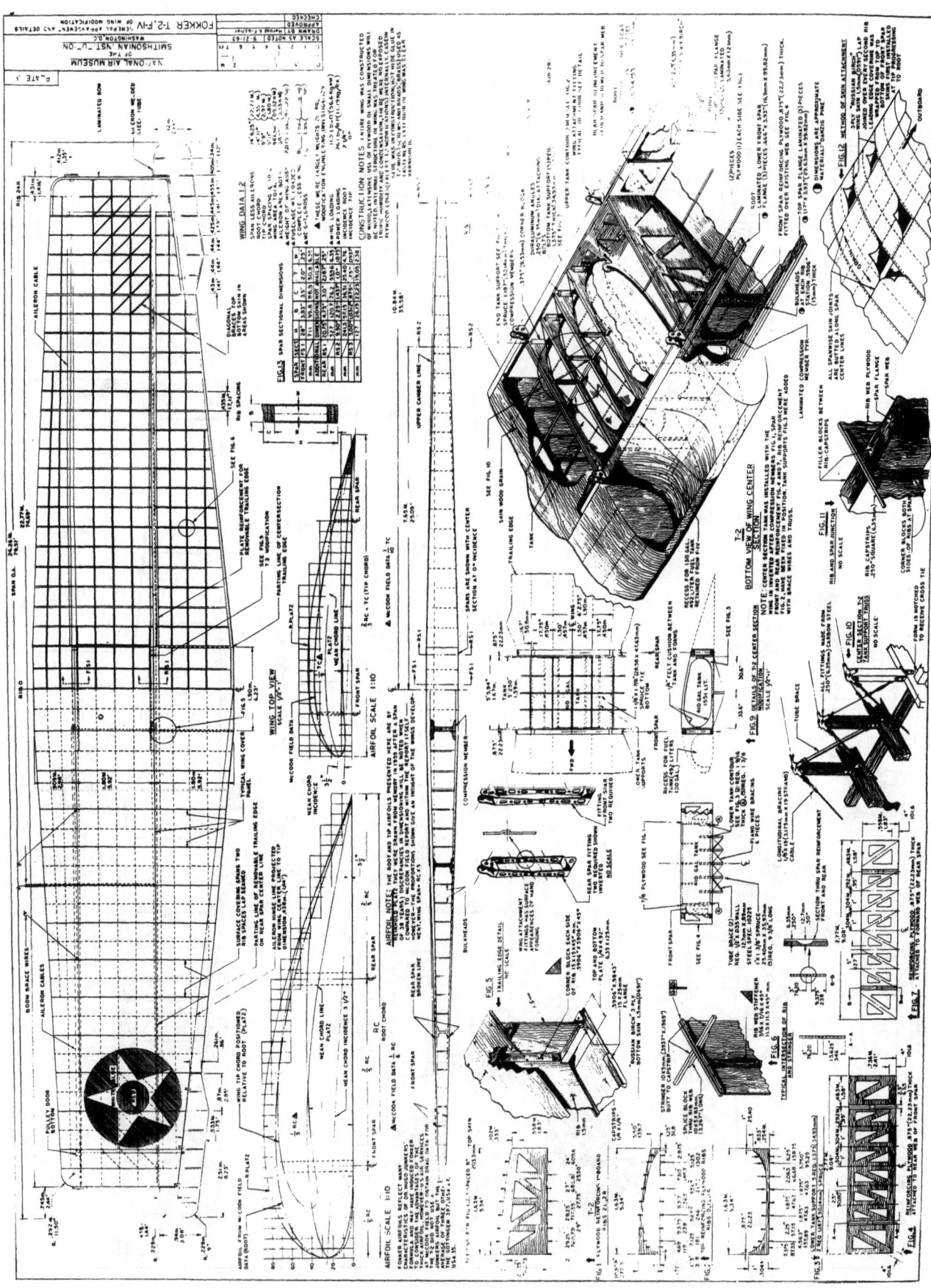

Figure 22.—Fokker T-2 F-IV, general arrangement and details of wing modification.

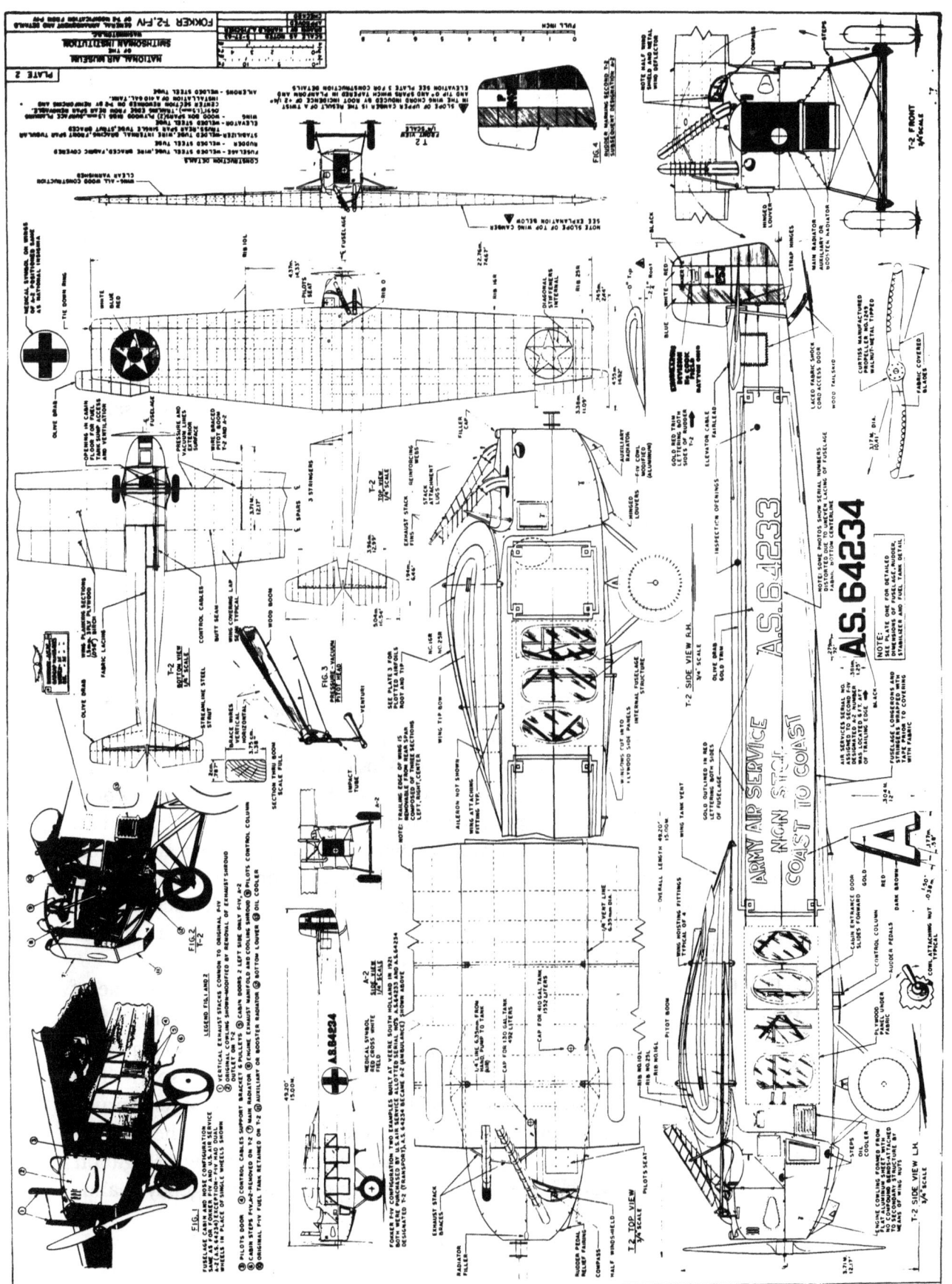

Figure 23.—Fokker T-2 F-IV, general arrangement and details of T-2 modification from F-IV.

The standard wheels and tires were found to be totally inadequate for the project and were replaced with standard Martin Bomber 44 x 10 wheels and 6-ply tires. The latter, used instead of the standard 13-ply tires, reduced the weight by about 20 pounds.

The empennage embodies balanced control surfaces constructed of steel tubing with fabric covering. The horizontal stabilizer is mounted directly to the upper surface of the fuselage and is rigidly braced by two streamlined tubes extending upward at an angle from the lower longerons.

Modifications to the fuselage were required for the coast-to-coast flight. The fuselage was stripped of all fabric and seats, and the cabin access doors were removed. The windows were replaced with large oval windows of celluloid, and a lightweight sliding door was installed at the rear left side of the cabin. An additional set of controls, and also bracing for the 185-gallon fuel tank, were welded in place. A special seat with folding back was fitted for the forward pilot and a bench (hammock) seat was provided in the rear of the cabin. The overall length of fuselage plus rudder is 49 feet 1 inch, the rectangular cross section of the fuselage has a maximum 74-inch width with full taper to the rudderpost.

Engines

The engines were the standard Liberty V-12 manufactured by the Ford Motor Company and Buick. They were overhauled, fitted with new cylinders, an 8-volt Delco ignition system, and Mosler M-1 spark plugs. During postoverhaul runs, tests were conducted to determine a setting which would give a minimum fuel consumption consistent with smooth engine operation. After runup testing, the engine was further checked for compression pressure, valve timing, tappet clearance, breaker timing for gap, and final adjustments made for service. The engine controls and their location are illustrated in figure 19. Today a Model-A Liberty engine (Air Service no. A68062, mfg. [Buick] no. B607) is installed in the airplane.

The fuel system was revised to connect in two additional tanks, one of 410-gallon capacity in the wing center section and one of 185 gallons in the fuselage. The standard 130-gallon gravity feed tank is located in a pocket in the leading edge of the wing center section, forward of the main spar. The 410-gallon tank in the wing center section is supported by seven spruce beams shaped to fit the tank. In operation fuel is pumped by the engine-driven Sylphon (bellows) pump from the two large tanks to the 130-gallon gravity tank, from which it is fed to the carburetor. An emergency manually operated wobble-pump is incorporated in the system along with strainers, primer and pressure gauge.

A 40-gallon reserve oil tank was installed in the fuselage between the firewall and the cabin fuel tank and directly behind the engine. In addition, an oil radiator was installed. The system was filled with Pennzoil triple extra heavy duty oil for the endurance flight and Triolene special extra heavy for the second nonstop flight attempt.

The standard cooling system is modified to include a reserve water tank in the cabin. An auxiliary radiator, equipped with shutters, is installed on the forward underside of the nose in parallel with the standard radiator.

Genealogy of the T–2

The Constructors

As in the planning and executing of this historic flight, two dominant personalities were associated with the construction of the T–2 (F–IV): the well-publicized Anthony H. G. "Tony" Fokker (1890–1939) and his chief constructor, Reinhold Platz (1886–). Fokker is now a legendary figure, having acquired much public notice from World War I and his subsequent exploits. The son of Dutch parents, Anna Hugona Wouterina (Diemont) Fokker and Herr Herman Fokker, he was born in Kediri, Java, on April 6, 1890. He constructed his first airplane without ever having seen one, and thereafter proceeded to teach himself to fly in 1910. He received his international flying license (FA–188) in 1911. During the next twenty years he tested each new Fokker aircraft design personally. His efforts to interest the Netherlands, the United States and Britain in his airplanes met with little success, but with the outbreak of World War I, he found a ready market in Germany.

The many designs produced by his factories were used with considerable success by the Germans during World War I. The famed DR–1 triplane and the D-VII were major contenders in that conflict. The D-VIII fighter designed near the end of the conflict in fact might be called the predecessor of the T–2.

In addition to his production of airplanes, Fokker was a bit of a philosopher, as indicated in the following extracts (pp. 266–273) from *The Flying Dutchman* by Fokker and Gould:*

> Experience is a dear school, but it is my contention that wise men as well as fools can learn in it. The chief reason why I am still of value today in the aeronautical industry is because I can make every part of a plane with my own hands if it should be necessary. It is fifteen years since I stood up to a draughting board, but I know exactly what I want, and if others' drawings do not suit me, I can point out specifically what is wrong, and to what degree. The woods

---

*See Bibliography.

Figure 28.—F-IV—T-2, 1922.

Figure 29.—F-IV—T-2, 1923.

Figure 26.—F-II, 1919.

Figure 27.—F-III, 1921.

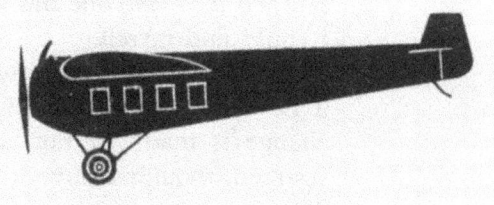

Figure 25.—F-1 (proposal).

Figure 24.—D-VIII, 1918.

are full of good, conventional plans for airplanes drawn by boys fresh from college. In their general outlines, it would be difficult to improve on them. What they miss are all the fine points learned only by practical experience in operating aircraft.

In certain departments of construction I am still more or less a layman. Happily, experts for stress analysis, specifications for materials, chemical formulae, and the more complicated branches of aerodynamics are more or less plentiful. But some of my best engineers make designs which are entirely impractical. A few imperfections can ruin an airplane for practical use.

Unlike a great many designers I actually fly my planes, use them as other men use automobiles and yachts. This experience I have utilized. There is a definite reason why every part was made in just that way, for every good airplane is the result of infinite compromises with aeronautic theory.

An investigator would find that I never built the fastest commercial or military plane, the lightest or the cheapest one, but in the long run our planes have given satisfaction, good service, and closely filled the demands made on them. Other planes, which excelled specifically in one way, such as greater speed, larger capacity, have fallen lamentably short in too many other ways to really be useful. That is why, over a long period of years, the reputation of the Fokker planes is today higher than ever. I will never build a freak plane.

Returning from a trip in one of my planes, I know what the problems of the mechanics are in servicing it, what the pilot's viewpoint is, and what the passenger thinks about its comfort and inconvenience. I have been sitting in the plane, getting in and out, watching others, observing my own reactions, and I must say this of myself, I have always been willing to criticize constructively my own work. Nothing I have yet done has ever really satisfied me. No one has yet found as many flaws in an airplane of mine as I could find myself.

Any of my engineers or workmen can argue with me, or criticize my planes if he thinks something should be different. If he can convince me, the change is made; if not, I appreciate his interest. I dislike flatterers or yes-men, though I have a number of employees who believe I like flattery. They are kept, however, for their good points, judged by their performance alone. I have had so much experience with personnel, putting persons in the wrong places and finding that they did better in others, that I have finally obtained some judgment about men. Particularly have I learned not to expect more out of people than they customarily give. I don't expect any man to give more than eighty percent of what he should in a job; in fact, I have found that if a workman does sixty percent of what he could do, it is a good average.

The same is true of myself. I seldom work at hundred percent efficiency. I constantly slip up, fail to do things on time, but my average seems to have been high enough for sound achievement. If I had not made so many mistakes, I can see that I would have been much more successful, for one not only does the wrong thing often, but fails to grasp the opportunity of doing the right thing, which in the end is the chief secret of success, I believe.

All my life I have been something of a lone wolf. Neither in Germany nor America have I been particularly popular among my competitors. Very often, others cannot see why one is successful, or in what manner one manages to beat them. I have always felt hated, not personally, because I do not know many of my competitors, but generally, as a force.

On the other hand I think most of my employees either like or admire me. This is true, especially of those with whom I worked side by side for years. They have learned to understand my ways, make allowances for my idiosyncrasies as I do for their little quirks, and know that I try to be just. They know that I appreciate them and their work, in spite of the fact that I drive them, and sharply criticise their results. More than ninety men have been with me over nine years, and ten over fifteen. None of them is under contract, and all have been approached by competitors. Some took more attractive offers, but most of them came back, and I found them even more loyal afterwards. They learned that everyone has something to complain about, but that by working for one man they had appreciation and contact, and were treated with at least human justness. In some of my employees I have implicit confidence, but I cannot say that I have a nature for making personal friends.

The real payment I have had out of life is not the money I have acquired but the sheer satisfaction of winning a fight. Just doing something which was hard gave me all the kick I needed. Money is only interesting as a source of power. If I could control a hundred million dollars I would like to do so, merely as raw material, a tool, a necessity of the game, to see how well I could organize a business and what could be got in the way of more power.

In the end, I suppose it is all vanity. In Germany I wanted my products to gain proper recognition. I have heard people say that I liked publicity and notoriety. That may be true to a certain extent. Certainly one wants acknowledgment of one's success. If one were alone in the world, one wouldn't start making a big hill which nobody would see. But if there were people around to watch the operation, and still others trying to make a bigger hill, there would be some incentive in making the biggest. Regardless of what men are after, money, fame, or just publicity, basically their purpose is the same, to fight to show their superiority. The usual measuring stick of success in this world is money, so that is what people fight for. Artists are living for fame, not money, but in business one cannot get fame without money, for that is the synonym for success. But my own satisfaction lies in the way I do a thing, and the fact that I have done it against odds.

As long as there is something new to fight for, I am happy. That in the end is what gives real satisfaction, for if things run along so smoothly that anyone could attend to them, the fun is gone out of them.

In a report dated Nov. 1, 1922,* Brig. Gen. Wm. Mitchell makes the following observation:

Mr. Fokker's success in building aircraft is largely due to his ability as a pilot and his first-hand knowledge of the desirable characteristics of control and stability in any type concerned. This ability to test any type and to recognize and rectify immediately the control system fault throughout is invaluable. His direct control over his factory and over his business, his large amount of first-hand knowledge and experience with all different types, plus his ability to pilot and test out his own types, gives him a decided advantage over most modern designers.

In a large measure, our own lack of success in the immediate solution of controlability problems has been due to the fact that designers have not ascertained the feel of the machine from a pilot's standpoint, and thus have to engage themselves with empirical values derived from control surface coefficients, averaged up from all the various types in general use, supplemented by the opinions of pilots who have flown their various types.

Unless one flies, this is the only natural method of ascertaining this data because our knowledge of control surface design from a standpoint of scientific aerodynamical data is not reliable enough for practical application and is too involved to give satisfactory results. In other words, our methods in designing control surfaces have been really rule of thumb while Mr. Fokker has used the cut and try system until he procured what he desired.

On the whole, approximately 8,000 Fokker machines have been built to date, and no master criticisms have been made against his type of construction by European designers except in prejudicial fashion. These were directly attributable to lack of experience with his methods. The ease with which any or all of his aircraft can be repaired or maintained has never been surpassed by any other type.

The simplicity of the application of his detailed structural ideas throughout all his types eliminates any complicated fittings and has contributed largely toward aiding Mr. Fokker and his organization to bring out new types very quickly.

In the course of constructing many aircraft (approximately 7000 during the war alone) Fokker technicians developed the autogenous welding (oxyacetylene welding) to a fine art in the construction of steel-tube fuselages. While frowned upon officially, through some special dispensation Fokker continued to develop this type of structure. The second important technical feature about Fokker aircraft was the wing structure which embodied a very deep camber airfoil together with box-structure spars, the structure entirely of wood including the covering material. The details of these two features have been described more fully in chapter 4 (p. 33).

---

* See Bibliography, Air Service, "Report of European Trip."

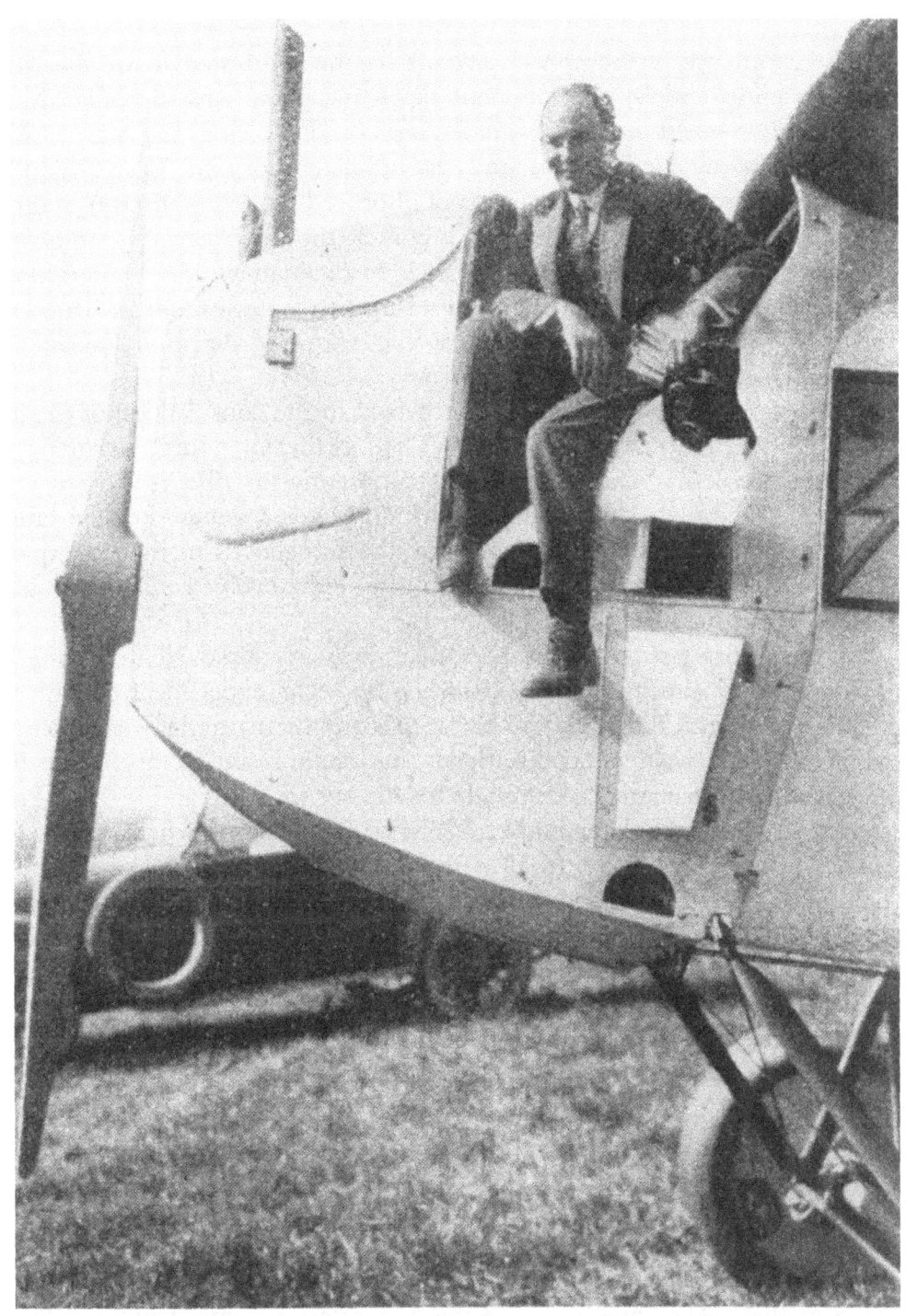

Figure 30.—Anthony Fokker on completion of test flight of F-IV.

The excellence of the D-VII aircraft has been attested to by the Allied combat pilots and by the fact that this same plane was the only aircraft specifically named in the Armistice terms. Following the war, Fokker returned to the Netherlands and set up his factory at Veere, island of Walcheren, from which a succession of improved models of aircraft, military as well as civilian, were produced. Figure 30 shows Fokker as he completed the test flight of the F-IV (T-2). In 1922 Fokker came to the United States, where he later became a citizen and set up two factories, one of which was in the New York area. Mourned by the aviation fraternity, Fokker died December 23, 1939, in New York City.

The second and equally important person in the construction of the T-2 was Reinhold Platz, who was born in Cottbus, Brandenburg, Germany, on January 16, 1886. While working as an apprentice in a Berlin oxygen plant he learned the metalsmith trade, and in 1904 the inventor Fouché taught him the technique of welding metals by the autogenous method. Expanding upon his earlier training under Fouché, Platz evolved many new techniques by his own welding experiments.

After a short term in military service he was employed in setting up welding plants until the year 1911, when he began experimenting with the welding of aircraft fuselages and parts. Shortly thereafter he was employed by Fokker as a welder-metalsmith at the Johannisthal factory. The first welded tubing structures were made for Fokker in 1912, and in 1913 Platz moved to the new Fokker plant at Schwerin, Germany, where he became master of the metalshop. In 1914 the authorities, as a result of structural failures, forbade the welded tube construction in aircraft. Only at Fokker, by demonstration of sufficient strength, was this type of structure permitted to be used in the construction of German military aircraft.

In 1915 a new test facility was organized by Fokker, and Platz was placed in charge of it. In 1916 he began taking an active part in the designing of aircraft and became the chief constructor of the Fokker works. At this time he began the calculations of strength for his first biplane with cantilever wood wings. This led to the design of some forty different types of aircraft, among which were the finest German fighters of World War I, including the DR-1 triplane (V-2, or experimental plane no. 2), the Fokker D-VII (V-11), the D-VIII (V-26), and the transport F-II (V-45). All these were constructed in the period 1917 to 1920. After the war and the move of the Fokker operations to the Netherlands, many training planes, sport planes, and a glider were constructed.

In 1921 with the move of the Fokker works to Veere on the island of Walcheren, Netherlands, Platz became director of the Fokker works and de-

Figure 31.—The Fokker Singing Society serenades at the tenth anniversary of "Platz" Veere (Netherlands), 1921. 1) Fokker; 2) Platz; 3) Mrs. Platz; 4) Business Manager Korner; 5) Holland-Dutch draftsman; 6 & 7) Two German master craftsmen; and other workmen on F-IV.

signed and constructed the larger commercial aircraft, bomber and torpedo planes, as well as a few gliders. While with Fokker at Veere, Platz designed the F-IV transport. Until the year 1922 he had only one draftsman and one technician in the design office. In the experimental shops one foreman and twenty skilled craftsmen translated the designs into prototypes. Between 1924 and 1931 he was promoted to the overall technical direction of the Fokker works in Amsterdam. His career did not end here for he served in technical directorate capacities during World War II and has very kindly supplied much factual information for this publication. From his biographical data, and from statements by others in a position to know the details (see Appendix 2), it is apparent that Reinhold Platz should receive much of the credit for the design of the T-2 (F-IV).

In his correspondence, Platz makes it very clear that he had no formal training in engineering and worked out all the stress analysis of these many designs by empirical methods. Fokker planes, both commercial and military types, found ready acceptance in many countries during the 1920's and early 1930's, including Britain, Germany, Austria, Argentina, Bolivia, Cuba, Finland, Denmark, France, Italy, Switzerland, and the United

Figure 32.—Fokker D-VIII, test illustrating structural strength of the Fokker cantilever wing.

States. In some countries other manufacturers were licensed to manufacture aircraft of Fokker design. In 1941 Platz was placed in charge of the construction of the V-1 and in 1945 directed the testing school at Aldershof.

The tremendous contribution of Platz to the success of the Fokker enterprises is best described by a letter written by A. L. Weyl (see Appendix 2, p. 86) appearing in *The Aeroplane, An Historical Survey* by Charles H. Gibbs-Smith.

The Aircraft

While all the aircraft preceding the T-2 might be regarded as the progenitors of this famous airplane, the D-VIII (V-26) of 1918, was the type for which the full-cantilever monoplane wing was designed. Additionally, Reinhold Platz has stated in letters to the author that the T-2 wing was in fact a geometric enlargement of the D-VIII wing. The tremendous strength of this wing is shown quite graphically by figure 32. Basically the wing was of two-spar construction, the spars running parallel and unbroken from tip to tip. The spars were of built-up box construction; plywood ribs

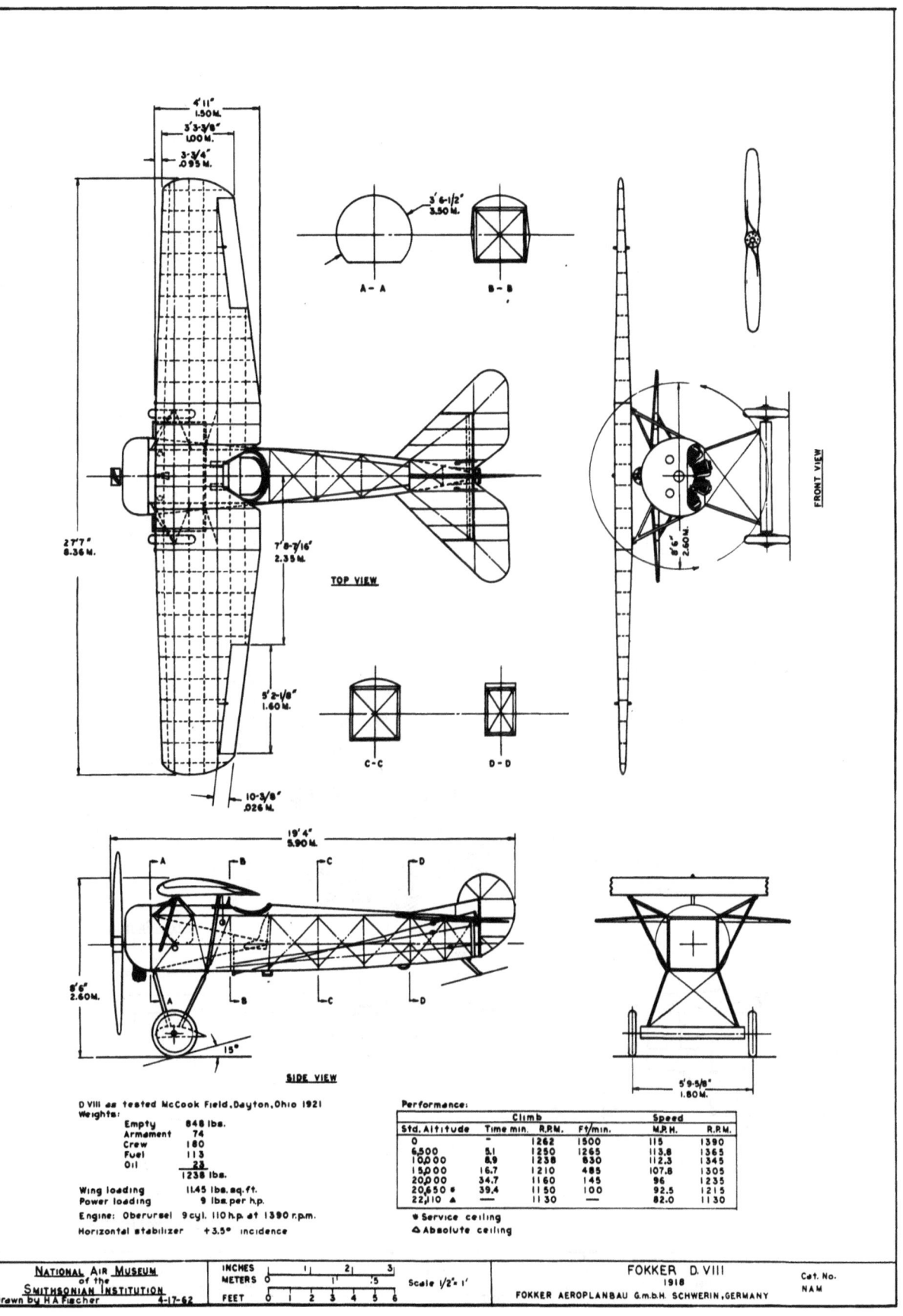

Figure 33.—Drawing of D-VIII.

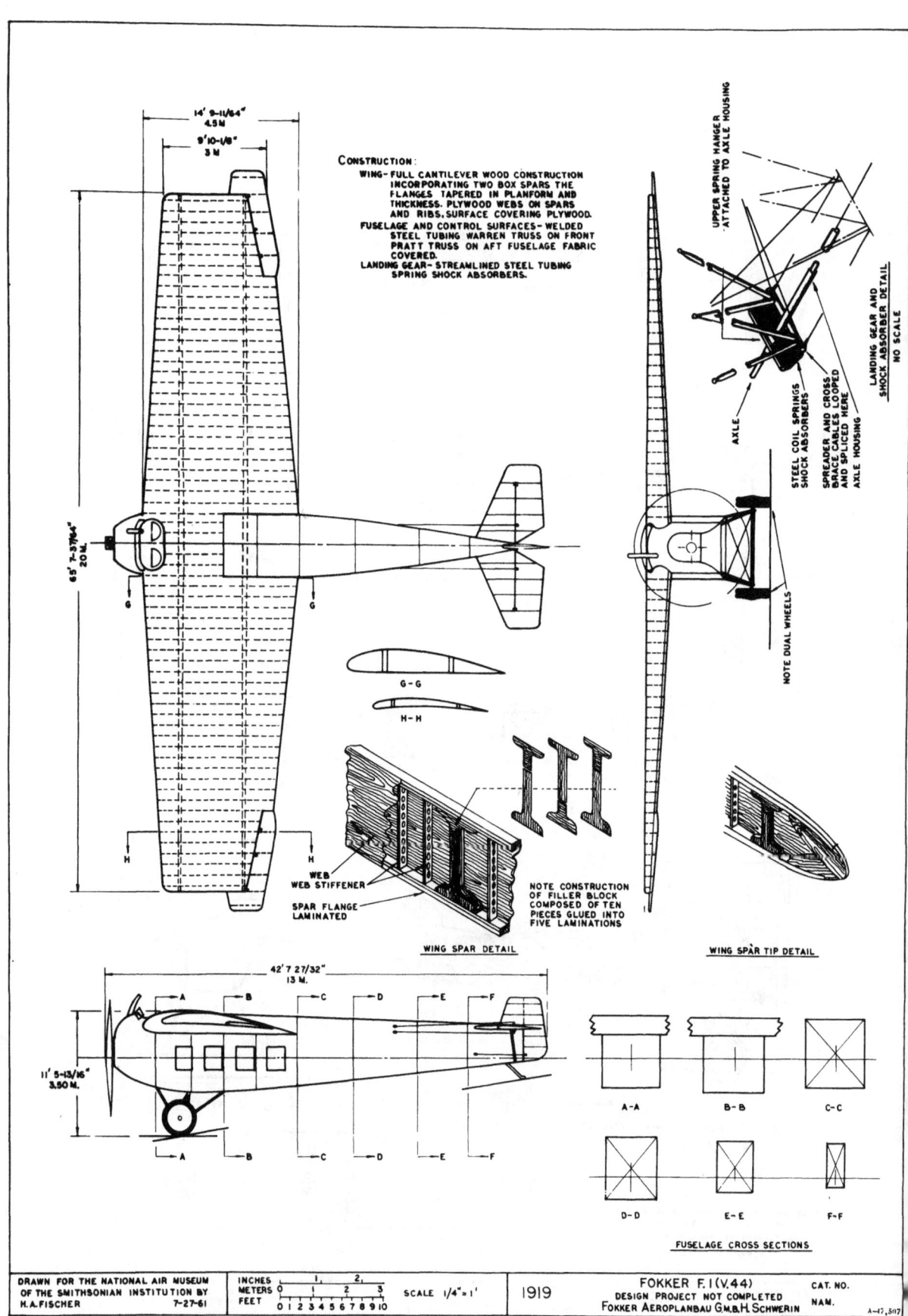

Figure 34.—Configuration of the proposed F-I (V-44).

of deep camber were attached by wood flanges glued and nailed in position, and all fitting points were reinforced by extra wood plates.

The D-VIII airplane, because of its clean, unbraced, full-cantilever wing became known as the "flying razor" during the closing weeks of World War I and, powered by the 140-hp Oberusal engine, was credited with 200 kph (124 mph) at sea level. It was designed for a German government competition and, like its predecessor the D-VII, emerged victorious. It appeared that the D-VIII would replace the D-VII and hold its own against contemporary Allied fighters; however, a requirement for strengthening the rear spar, a result of static tests, delayed construction. A series of accidents resulted in suspension of production and, as a consequence of the delay, only about 36 D-VIII's reached the fighting squadrons prior to the Armistice. Experience proved that the original spar construction, as designed, was correct. The monoplane wing and clean fuselage gave the pilot an almost uninterrupted field of view. The wing was attached by two fixed struts plus two adjustable struts, shown in the drawing (fig. 33).

The F-I (V-44) was a design proposal which did not become a reality. The aircraft was to embody the cantilever monoplane wing and a passenger-carrying fuselage. In the course of construction it became evident that passengers could enter only with great difficulty. The open fuselage was scrapped. Only a sketch of the proposed configuration has been located, and is included here as figure 34. The wing was constructed and, with a new fuselage design, became the V-45 prototype of the F-II. Figure 35 shows this first Fokker model designed and completed as a transport.

The F-II (V-45) of 1919, was constructed in Schwerin, Germany, in that

Figure 35.—Fokker V-45, prototype of the Fokker F-II.

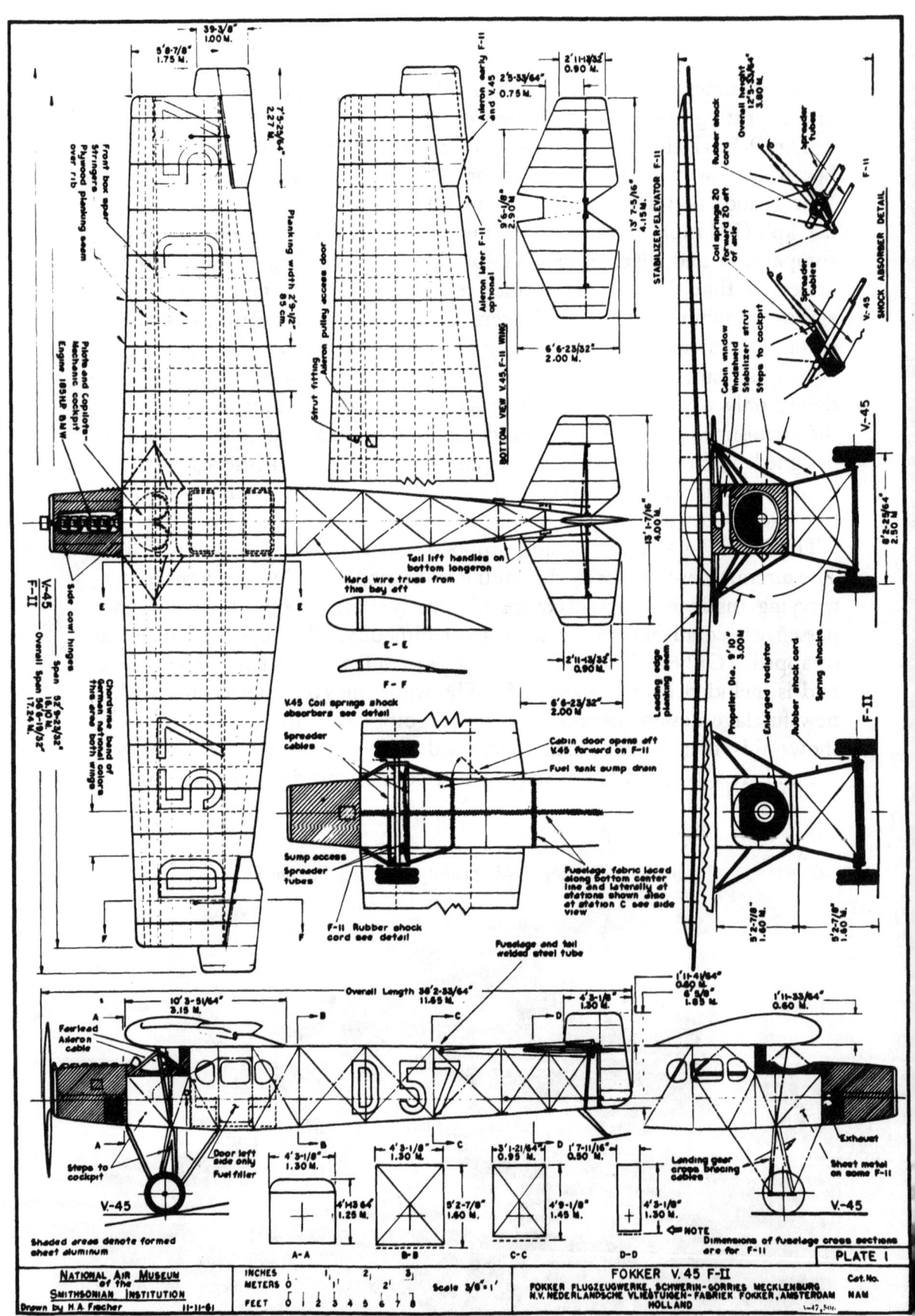

Figure 36.—Drawing of V-45—F-II.

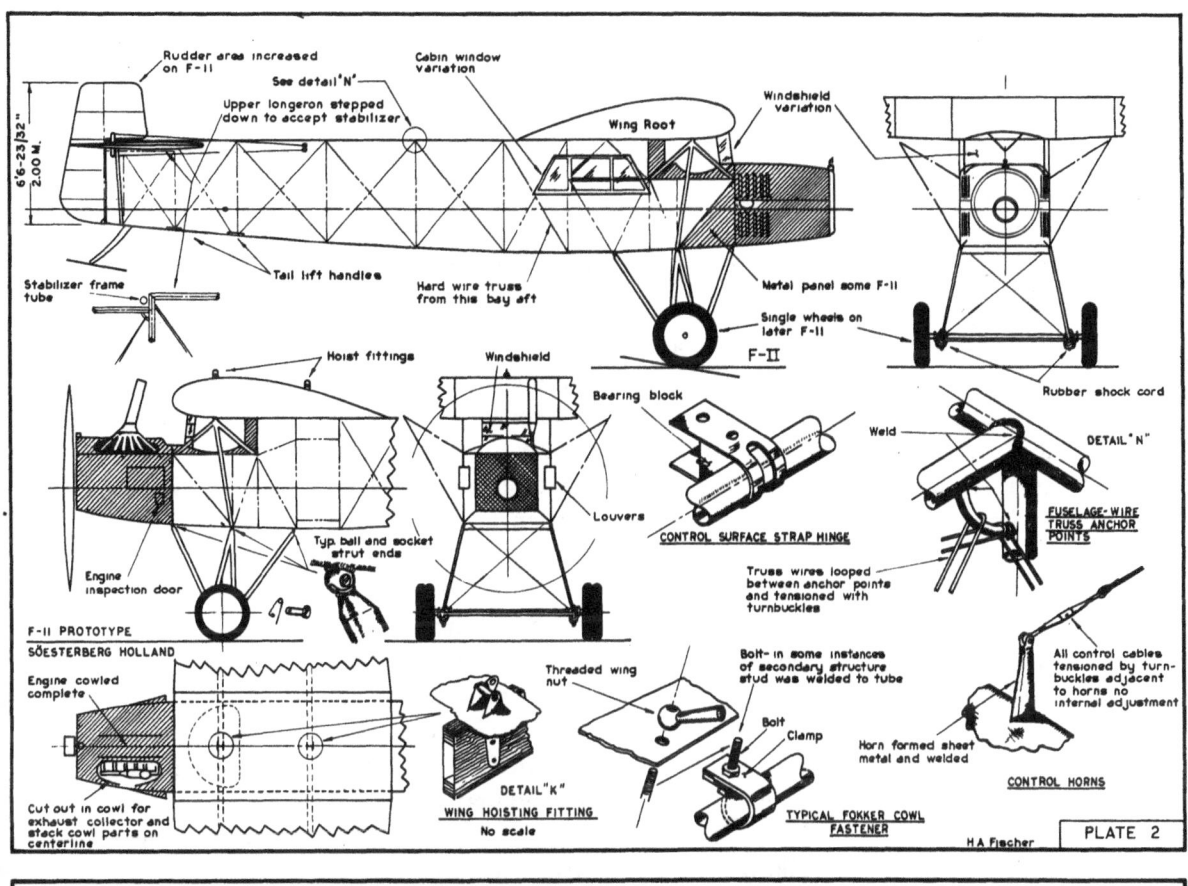
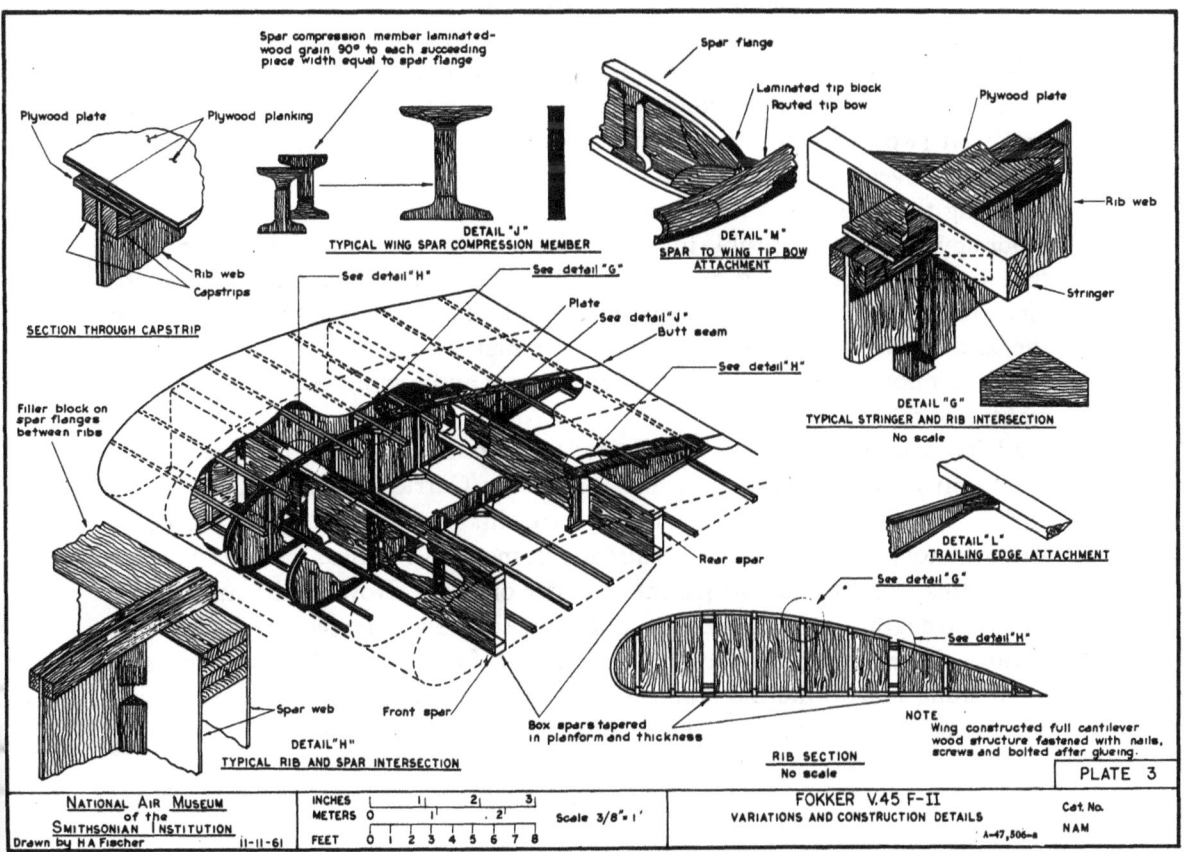

Figure 37.—Fokker V-45—F-II. Variations and constructions details.

year and flown by the test pilot Parge. It proved to be very stable, so stable in fact that it could not be looped. Powered by a 185-hp BMW engine, this airplane made one test flight with nine persons on board.

The transfer of the V-45 to the Netherlands from Germany after the war is a story in itself. It is related here by Reinhold Platz, in a letter to the author, March 2, 1958:

>Some days after Fokker was advised of the success of the test flights, came a telephone call: This is the Niederlaendischerhof Hotel. A foreigner would like to speak to a gentleman from the Fokker factory here at the hotel, would that be possible? I suspected it might be somebody interested or perhaps even a buyer and quickly went to the hotel room of the foreigner. Judging from his looks, he could have been taken for an Indian. "Do you know me?" he asked with a peculiar German accent. "I have never seen you in all my life," I answered him. He then removed his black whiskers from his upper lip, and I would have given anything to have given Bernard de Waal (Fokker pilot) a big bear hug. Without a word being said, it was clear what the object of his visit was. It was now a question of taking the air police unware and making it possible to build the forbidden plane. "The working council" (Trade Union) had to be let into the secret. I knew that Wichmann could be a very important man. The second man in the "Work Council," the "Upholstery master" was Boelkow, the father of the now very well known aviation engineer Boelkow from Stuttgart. Also the motor specialist Duengel had to cooperate. The parties concerned all knew and appreciated de Waal.
>
>My plan: Notify Wichmann, Boelkow, Duengel; de Waal is here. He wants to fly the F-II and take it with him. We can take orders from Holland and wait (we were all interested in keeping the factory busy). I must go to Berlin this evening, in order not to have anything to do with it. De Waal will be flying the F-II tomorrow morning. Wichmann and Boelkow, you two as labor advisors are responsible for this: "Notifying the airpolice and seeing to it that de Waal does not leave the landing field." Duengel should have the airplane in good condition. The start should take place in the hangar, so that the airpolice will not suspect anything at first. I was clearly informed; de Waal was notified. We also procured him a hand sewing machine which he wanted to take along.
>
>I left that evening for Berlin and hoped for success. The next day, I left on the first train back to Schwerin, which passed by Gorries airfield. The airfield and the hangars were clearly seen from the train. It seemed to have succeeded. In the factory the excitement was already tremendous. Since I was responsible for all this I had to go and see the minister of state. Now Wichmann was to be my strength and support. As labor advisor he was feared, he looked like Stalin. After giving my lecture (accounting for what had happened) and mentioning that to me the labor advisor was the best guarantee that nothing adverse could happen, the minister began to criticise the conduct of the labor

counselor. This was what Wichmann was waiting for. He hit the minister's table with his iron fist, so that everything that was on it flew in the air, and thundered so loudly, that the minister, out of fear, quickly changed, and soon thereafter, quite politely allowed us to leave. To our joy, the way Wichmann had come forward had quickly smoothed everything.

Unfortunately, de Waal's flight did not go smoothly. He said to me when we met, "The crate was wonderful, but I had motor trouble and I had to make a forced landing on good ground in Germany. After a short while, another forced landing, still in Germany. I was working on the motor, when suddenly two policemen (state patrol officers) stood by the airplane and wanted to know from where I came and where I was heading for. I tried to explain to them in Dutch I did not understand German—that I must have wrongly flown out of Holland. Since they did not know what to advise, one of them went to the city hall (I no longer recall of which town) to be told what to do with me. Meanwhile, I kept on inspecting my motor and after it seemed to be in order, I signaled to the officer who had remained with me and asked him if he could turn the propeller for me. He did so, the motor started, I told him to stand aside, and went off. I had to make a third forced landing in Holland, unfortunately, with major damage. Shortly after talking to Fokker, he was on the site, and in spite of the damage, he was delighted with the machine."

The last portion of this "transfer" was by boat due to the damage incurred in the landing. The V–45—F-II was purchased by the National Research Service for use as a flying laboratory.

The F-II became the first of the transports operated in Europe, entering service on April 17, 1920. It was used primarily in surveying of routes pioneered by KLM (Koninklijke Luchtvaart Maatschappij) Royal Dutch Airlines. These routes were surveyed by two F-II's registration numbers HNABC and HNABD. The first Fokker commercial aircraft (HNABD) to fly to England crossed the channel on Sept. 30, 1920. *The Times* of London hailed the F-II as the "plane of the future." German Aero Lloyd also operated several machines of this type.

Technically the F-II was of similar construction to the D-VIII and V–45. It had the full-cantilever wing constructed of plywood, the "elephant ear" ailerons (a distinctive feature of the D-VII), and the steel-tube fuselage (fabric covered). Accommodations were provided for six passengers protected from the elements by an enclosed cabin of doubtful comfort, while the pilot remained in an exposed cockpit, immediately behind the engine. A seventh passenger could be seated beside the pilot. This aircraft design was the first Fokker airplane to have stress calculations verified by engineering methods. These were carried out by Dipl. Ing. Bethage of the German

Testing Institute prior to the airplane's entering passenger service. This computation failed to show any over or under strength. According to contemporary references, the airplane was powered by a 185-hp BMW engine and was credited with a maximum speed of 150 kph (93 mph) and cruising speed of 120 kph (75 mph).

The profiles and principal dimensions are shown in figure 37.

V-45 AND F-II, SUMMARY OF SPECIFICATIONS

	V-45	F-II
Span	16.1 m (52 ft 9^{2}%$_{32}$ in)	17.25 m (56 ft 7 in.)
Length	11.65 m (38 ft 2^{3}%$_{4}$ in)	11.65 m (38 ft 2^{3}%$_{4}$ in.)
Height	3.80 m (12 ft 5^{3}%$_{4}$ in)	3.8 m (12 ft 5^{3}%$_{4}$ in.)
Tread	2.5 m (8 ft 2^{2}%$_{4}$ in)	3.10 m (10 ft 4½ in.)
Wing area	42 sq m (434 sq ft)	38.2 m (411 sq ft)
Weight empty	1200 kg (2643 lb)	1190 kg (2690 lb)
Weight gross	1900 kg (4200 lb)	1884 kg (4150 lb)
Useful weight	700 kg (1543 lb)	694 kg (1526 lb)

Progress in air transport design was swift even in this embryonic period; evidence is the fact that the design of the F-III was begun even before the first F-II was delivered. Certain shortcomings in operating convenience, maneuverability, and economy of the F-II were remedied in the F-III. The new design, initiated in 1921, was based on a firm foundation of the many earlier successful designs. Fokker wanted to design this model entirely by himself.

No startling changes were made, though the passenger seating accommodations were improved, and servicing was simplified by the addition of a hand-operated wobble-pump which speeded the refueling operations. The pilot was provided with better visibility though he remained outside. The engine was displaced slightly off center to the left and the pilot's seat was placed to the right with a cutout in the wing's leading edge for the pilot's head. This cutout resulted in aerodynamic problems which were not easily remedied. Engine controls were mounted directly on the engine and essential instruments were placed in close proximity to the pilot, though an instrument panel, as such, was not among the refinements incorporated. The engine could be observed and minor adjustments could be made. The pilot's comfort was somewhat doubtful due to the heat of the engine on his left and the exposure to the elements on his right side. Structurally the aircraft was an enlargement and refinement of the F-II and was more maneuverable. KLM's London-Amsterdam service was opened on April 15, 1921, using the F-III's powered by the

Figure 38.—Anthony Fokker seated in Fokker F-III.

230-hp Siddeley "Puma" engine. Comfortable, bordering on plush, seating accommodations were provided for five passengers. With the "Puma" engine the maximum speed was reported to have been 169 kph with a cruising speed of 145 kph (90 mph). The similarity to the F-II is clearly shown in figures 39 and 40.

F-III, Summary of Specifications

Span................	17.60 m (57 ft 9 in.)
Length..............	10.3 m (33 ft 10 in.)
Height..............	3.2 m (10 ft 6 in.)
Tread...............	2.5 m
Wing area...........	39.1 sq m (421 sq ft.) (including ailerons)
Weight empty........	1267 kg (2815 lb.)
Gross weight.........	2034 kg (4520 lb.)
Maximum speed......	169 km (105 mph.)
Cruising speed.......	90 mph (145 mph.)

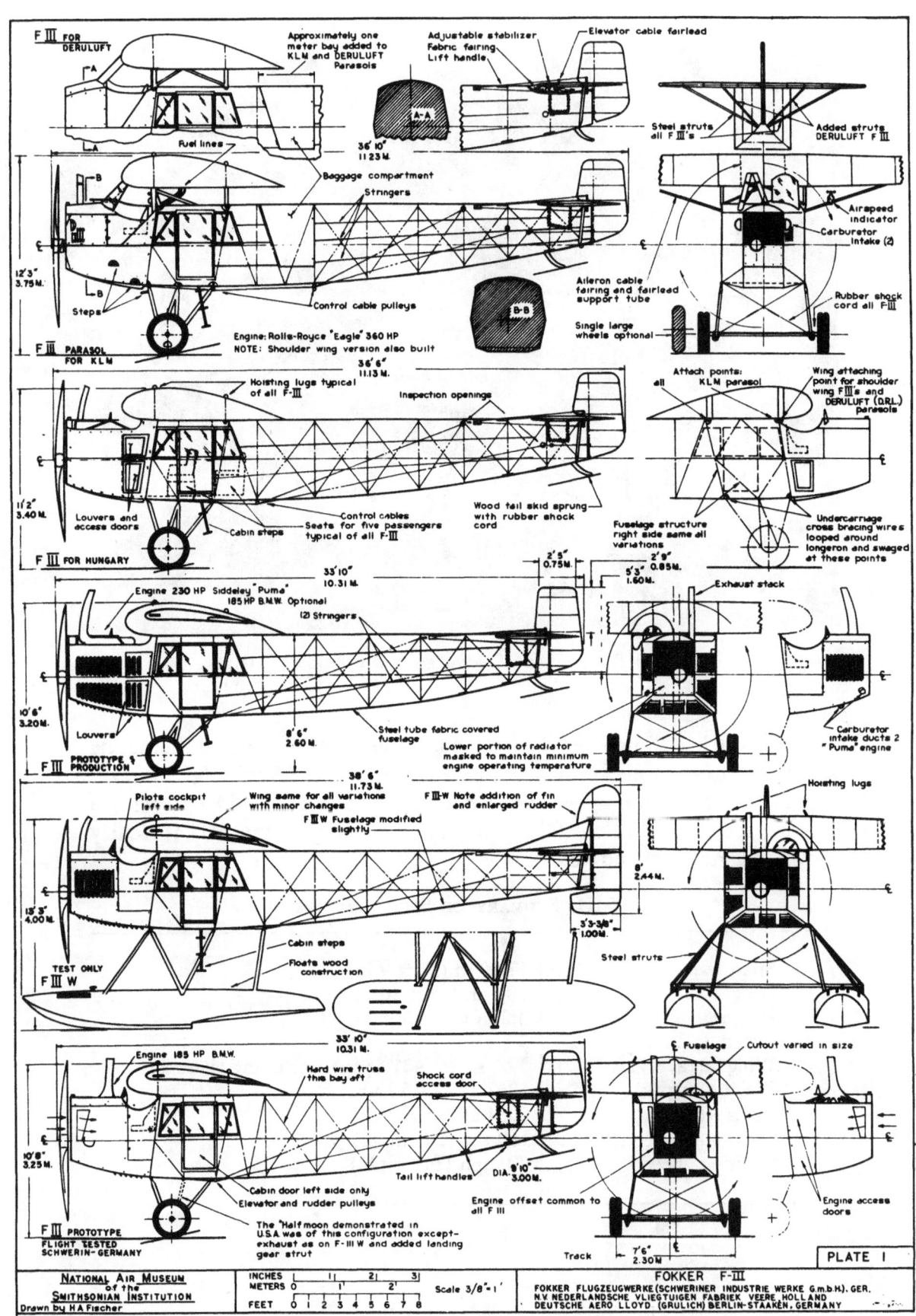

Figure 39.—F-III, Plan view and construction details.

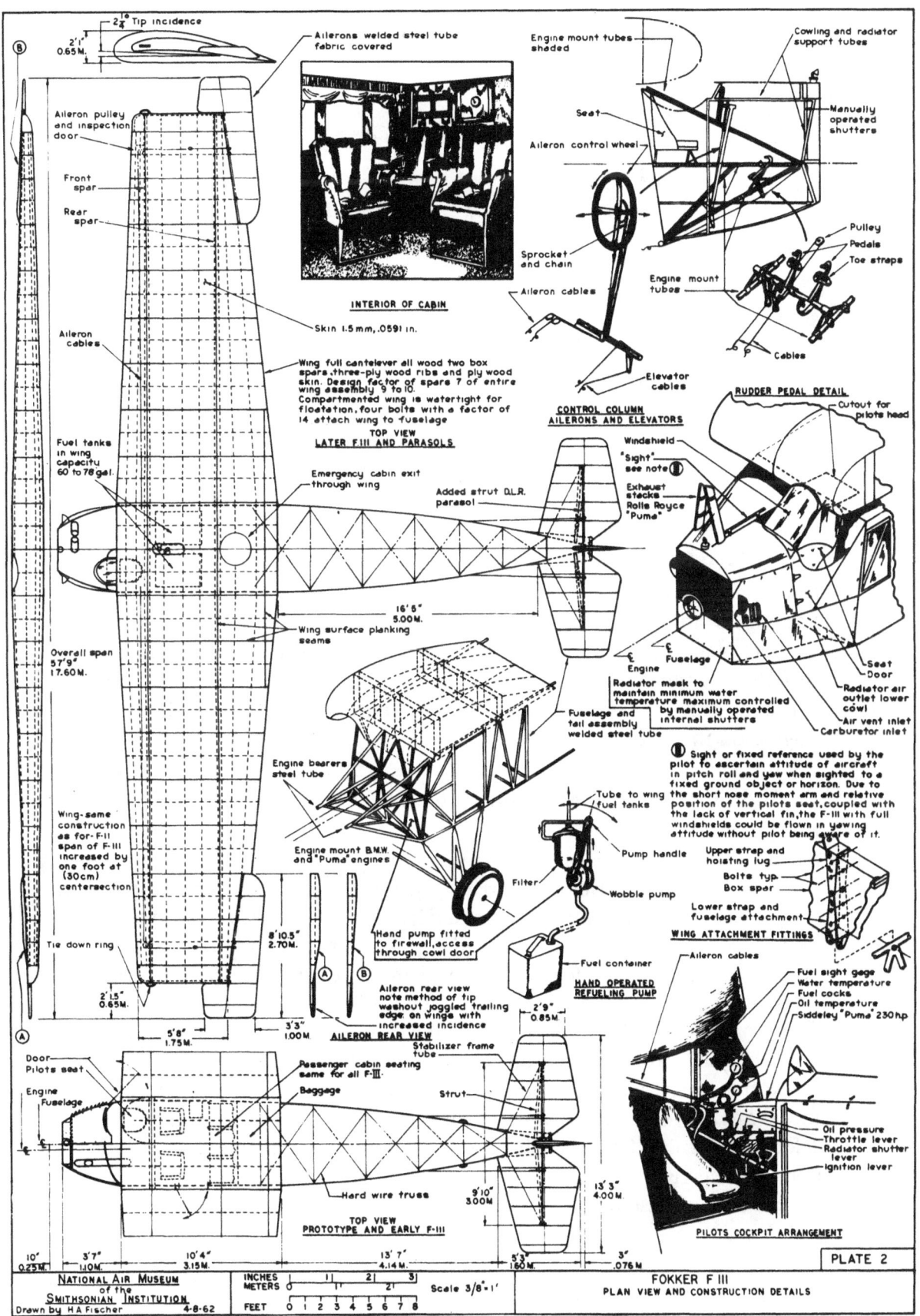

Figure 40.—F-III.

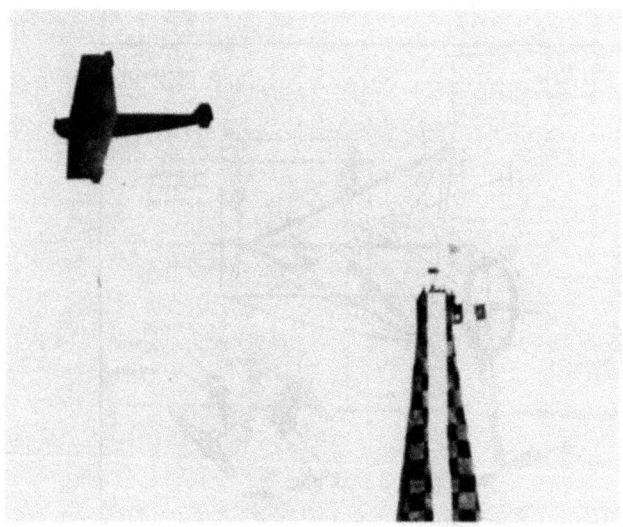

Figure 41.—Fokker Transport A-2 airplane, sister airplane of Transcontinental T-2, rounding pylon, at St. Louis races. October 4, 5, 6, 1923.

The F-IV, subject of this report, followed the basic concept of its predecessors. As originally conceived, the airplane was to have carried 8–10 passengers and a pilot. The passengers were afforded the comparative comfort of an enclosed cabin but the pilot remained outside, as in previous models. In this model the pilot cockpit was on the left side of the forward fuselage, with the Liberty, or 380-hp Rolls-Royce, or 450-hp Napier Lion engine on the right side.

Only two of this model were constructed and both were purchased by the U.S. Air Service under contract no. 344, dated June 30, 1922. These two planes became the T-2 (Air Service 64233) and the A-2 (Air Service 64234), the latter being fitted out as an ambulance plane, hence the A-2 designation. The static tests carried out by Lt. Dichman made use of the wing of the A-2, while the T-2 was undergoing flight-acceptance evaluation by Lt. Kelly. The A-2 was entered in the Detroit Aerial Contest of 1922 (Event no. 3, Air Race for Light Commercial Airplane), where it won 3rd place at an average speed of 90.7 mph for the 257.7 mile course (see fig. 41). The story of the A-2 following its conversion and use as an ambulance plane has been lost, but that of the T-2 has been sufficiently documented to make this report possible, though no formal log was prepared for it. The fact that Lt. Kelly was aboard the airplane on almost every flight either as pilot or passenger has made it possible to establish the details of its operations by referring to his personal logbook. We are indebted to Col. Kelly for extracting these details for our use.

Figure 42.—Fokker Transport T-2 over McCook Field.

The following flight log of the Air Service Fokker T-2 (fig. 39), McCook Field, no. P-253, has been extracted and edited from the pilot records of 1st. Lt. Oakley G. Kelly, A.S.:

FLIGHT LOG OF T-2, JUNE 1, 1922, TO JUNE 1, 1923

1922
June	1	Initial test flight	25 min
	2	Cooling test 4 passengers	1 hr 05 min
July	13	Cooling test with additional radiator	18 min
	15	Performance test	5 hr 20 min
	16	Performance test	1 hr 20 min
	19	Performance test climb 6000 ft	30 min
	20	Performance test	2 hr 00 min
Aug.	2	Performance test climb 6000 ft	51 min
	4	Performance test climb 10,200 ft	2 hr 00 min
	9	Motor test	15 min
	10	McCook Field to Wilbur Wright Field and return, Maj. Gen. Mason M. Patrick, passgr.	33 min

Total flying time to date 14 hr 37 min

FLIGHT LOG OF T-2, JUNE 1, 1922, TO JUNE 1, 1923—Continued

1922

Airplane now in shop being modified for transcontinental nonstop flight.

Sept.	13	Test airplane now designated T-2	14 min
	17	Test	30 min
	18	Test	1 hr 13 min
	19	Oakley G. Kelly, J. A. Macready, pilots; Chas. Dworack, assembly foreman and Clyde Reitz, airplane mechanic left McCook Field for San Diego, Calif. to prepare for attempted nonstop west-to-east flight.	
	19	McCook Field to Scott Field	4 hr 00 min
	21	Scott Field to Ft. Sill, Lawton, Okla.	5 hr 30 min
	22	Ft. Sill to Ft. Bliss, El Paso, Tex.	7 hr 40 min
	24	Ft. Bliss to Rockwell Field, San Diego, Calif.	7 hr 30 min
Oct.	2	Motor test at San Diego	35 min
	3	Flight test, San Diego	4 hr 30 min
		Total flying time to date	46 hr 19 min
	5–6	First attempt at nonstop flight blocked by fog in mountain pass near Banning, Calif. Returned to vicinity of San Diego and remained in the air to establish unofficial world's duration record	35 hr 18½ min
Nov.	3–4	Second attempt at nonstop flight: Take-off from Rockwell Field at 05-57 a.m. Nov. 3 and landed at Schoen Field, Ft. Harrison, Indianapolis, Ind. Failure due to cracked water jacket in engine cylinder and resulting loss of all coolant. Elapsed time	25 hr 30 min
	10	Indianapolis to McCook Field (new engine)	1 hr 15 min
	29	Motor test	11 min

1923

Feb.	8	Motor test	40 min
	17	Motor test	52 min
	23	Motor test	20 min
Mar.	1	Motor test	40 min
	7	Motor test	20 min
	14	Motor test	49 min
	27	Motor test	24 min
	30	To Wilbur Wright Field	15 min
		Total flying time to date	112 hr 53½ min

FLIGHT LOG OF T–2, JUNE 1, 1922, TO JUNE 1, 1923—Continued

1923

Mar.	30	Attempted to establish official world's distance and endurance record over measured closed course with high-compression engine. Flight failed when pilot inadvertently closed radiator-shutter control while adjusting parachute harness after pilots changed seats. Time of flight	7 hr 55 min
	31	Wright Field to McCook Field	15 min
Apr.	4	Motor test after engine change	1 hr 00 min
	6	Motor test	44 min
	7	Motor test	20 min
	9	Motor test	30 min
	10	Motor test	20 min
	16–17	Takeoff made from Wilbur Wright Field at 09:38 a.m., Apr. 16, 1923, and landing made at 09:42 p.m. Oct. 17 flight officially timed by Otis Porter, official timer for Indianapolis Speedway and Orville Wright designated as official observer.	

Official world's duration record established. 36 hr 4 min 8 sec
Official world's distance record 2,516½ miles.
Official world's record speeds for the following distances:

    1500 km avg speed 73.00 mph
    2000 " " 72.50 "
    2500 " " 71.98 "
    3000 " " 71.96 "
    3500 " " 71.15 "
    4000 " " 70.79 "

World's weight-lifting record 10,800 lb with one 400- hp Liberty 12 engine.

	18	Wright Field to McCook Field for engine change	31 min
	25	Motor test	22 min
	25	McCook Field to Bolling Field, Washington, D.C.	4 hr 20 min
	26	Bolling Field to Mitchel Field, Long Island	2 hr 25 min
	28	Motor test	1 hr 10 min
May	2	Mitchel Field to Roosevelt Field, Long Island	25 min
	2–3	Left Roosevelt Field, Long Island, at 12:36 p.m., e.s.t., May 2, 1923, and landed at Rockwell Field, San Diego, Calif., at 12:26 p.m., P.s.t., May 3, 1923, which established the first nonstop coast-to-coast airplane flight. Time	26 hr 50 min

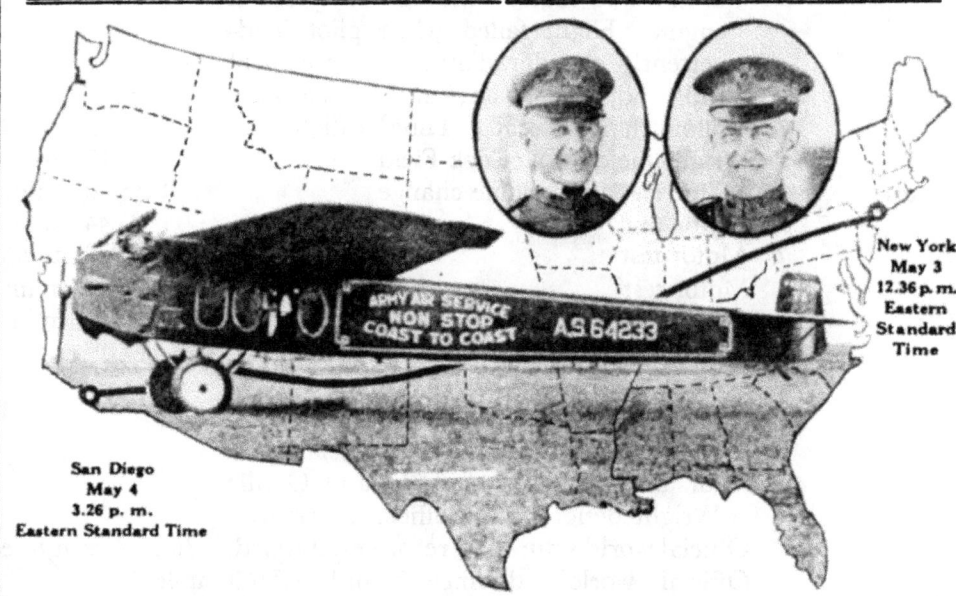

Figure 43.—Fokker T-2, 1923, nonstop, coast to coast, an advertisement for the Netherlands Aircraft Manufacturing Co.

FLIGHT LOG OF T–2, JUNE 1, 1922, TO JUNE 1, 1923—Continued

1923			
May	19	Flying escort for Army Transport U.S. Grant entering San Diego Harbor with Sec. of War John W. Weeks and 27 members of Congress	1 hr 10 min
	25	San Diego, Calif., to El Paso, Tex.	6 hr 30 min
	26	El Paso, Tex., to Lawton, Okla.	6 hr 10 min
	27	Lawton, Okla., to Kansas City, Mo.	4 hr 25 min
	28	Kansas City, Mo., to McCook Field, Dayton, Ohio	7 hr 15 min
June	1	Dayton, Ohio, to Bolling Field, Washington, D.C.	4 hr 00 min
		Total flying time to date	225 hr 35 min

Appendix

War Department, Air Service, Engineering Division,
Contract 344–T, June 30, 1922

WAR DEPARTMENT
AIR SERVICE, ENGINEERING DIVISION

Contract 344-T.

THIS CONTRACT, made and entered into this 30th day of June, 1922, by and between ANTHONY H. G. FOKKER, an individual of Amsterdam, Holland, hereinafter called the "Contractor", party of the first part, and the UNITED STATES OF AMERICA, hereinafter called the "Government", party of the second part, represented by R. H. FLEET, Captain, A. S., U. S. A., hereinafter called the "Contracting Officer", acting by direction of the Chief of Air Service, and under the authority of the Secretary of War, WITNESSETH:

WHEREAS, the parties hereto, did, on December 4, 1920, enter into Contract 344, wherein the Contractor agreed to design, manufacture and assemble for and deliver to the Government two (2) Fokker Single-seater Armored Combat Monoplanes, Type Cantilever Parasol, V-40, each designed and constructed to carry one 300-H.P. American-built Wright Hispano aircraft engine, and two (2) Fokker Transport Monoplanes, Type F-4, each designed and constructed to carry one Liberty 12-cylinder aircraft engine, for the total sum of $95,000.00; and

WHEREAS, the Contractor has satisfactorily completed the performance of Contract 344 and the Government has received, inspected and accepted all the said airplanes and has made settlement in full therefor;

NOW, THEREFORE, in consideration of said Contractor's hereby acknowledging satisfaction in full of any and all claims, both formal and informal, of whatsoever nature arising under or by virtue of, or in connection with said Contract 344, and all orders issued thereunder and hereby binding itself and its successors and assigns, to save harmless the Government from any and all claims of every kind or character whatsoever, both formal and informal, for material or labor furnished or expenses or obligations incurred, on account of said Contract 344, and all orders issued thereunder, the Government hereby acknowledges full and complete performance, on the part of said Contractor, of said Contract 344 and all orders issued thereunder, except that the provisions of Article VI of said Contract 344 are not hereby terminated but remain in full force and effect.

IN WITNESS WHEREOF, the parties hereto have executed this agreement in quintuplicate the day first hereinbefore written.

Witnesses:

ANTHONY H. G. FOKKER
BY R. B. C. NOORDUYN
HIS ATTORNEY-IN-FACT

UNITED STATES OF AMERICA

R. H. FLEET,
Captain, A.S., U.S.A.,
Contracting Officer.

WAR DEPARTMENT

AIR SERVICE, ENGINEERING DIVISION

Contract No. 344

THIS CONTRACT, made and entered into this 4th day of December, 1920, by and between ANTHONY H. G. FOKKER, an individual of Amsterdam, Holland, hereinafter called the "Contractor", party of the first part, and the UNITED STATES OF AMERICA, hereinafter called the "Government", party of the second part, represented by R. H. FLEET, Captain, A. S., United States Army, hereinafter called the "Contracting Officer", acting by direction of the Chief of Air Service, and under the authority of the Secretary of War.

WITNESSETH:

In consideration of the mutual covenants herein contained, the parties hereto agree as follows:

ARTICLE I

(1) The Contractor shall design, manufacture and assemble for and deliver to the Government in the manner, at the time and place and for the consideration hereinafter named, the following airplanes, hereinafter called the "articles"; viz.:

  (a) Two (2) Fokker Single-seater Armored Combat Monoplanes, Type Cantilever Parasol, V-40, each designed and constructed to carry one 300-H.P. American-built Wright Hispano aircraft engine; and

  (b) Two (2) Fokker Transport Monoplanes, Type F-4, each designed and constructed to carry one Liberty 12-cylinder aircraft engine.

(2) Each of the articles shall be designed, constructed, equipped and delivered in accordance with the specification for airplanes of its type attached hereto and hereby made a part hereof.

(3) The engines, propellers, tachometers and tachometer shafts enumerated in the two attached specifications as being furnished by the Government, shall be furnished by the Government to the Contractor, free of charge, f. o. b. Rotterdam, Holland, and each of such items of equipment shall be installed by the Contractor in the proper article and shall be so returned to the Government. All other equipment, materials and supplies required for the complete performance of this contract shall be furnished by the Contractor.

ARTICLE II

(1) Time is of the essence of this Contract.

(2) The articles shall be delivered by the Contractor to the Government, f. o. b. ship, Rotterdam, Holland, consigned to the Contracting Officer, suitably boxed and packed for overseas shipment, within five (5) months from the time when all of the equipment to be furnished by the Government under Section (3) of Article I is delivered to the Contractor.

ARTICLE III

The Contractor shall not be responsible for, or be deemed to be in default hereunder by reason of delays in the performance of this contract caused by strikes, fires, explosions, riots, acts of God, failure of transportation, or other causes beyond the control and without the fault of the Contractor, including delays caused to the Contractor by the direct act or failure to act of the Government, and the Contractor's time for performance of this contract shall hereby be extended to cover the delay in performance so caused to the Contractor; provided, that the Contractor shall have immediately and fully notified the Contracting Officer of any such cause of delay and shall have used his best efforts promptly to remove the same and to obviate the effects thereof; and provided further, that such delay shall not have been due to the Contractor's failure to comply with any of the provisions of this contract. The Contractor shall proceed with the performance of this contract as soon as, and to the extent that any such cause of delay shall have been removed.

ARTICLE IV

(1) Each of the articles shall be inspected in accordance with the requirements of this contract by a duly authorized representative of the Contracting Officer at the Contractor's factory in Holland prior to the acceptance thereof by the Government.

(2) If any article is rejected upon inspection for failure to comply with the requirements of this contract, the Contractor shall have a further period of one (1) month after such rejection to make said article fully comply therewith.

ARTICLE V

The Government shall pay the Contractor for the articles upon the delivery to, inspection and acceptance thereof by the Government, in accordance with the requirements of this contract, as follows:

(a) Eighteen Thousand Dollars ($18,000) in money of the United States of America, or its equivalent in money of the Netherlands Government, at the then rate of exchange, for each of the articles called for in sub-division (a) of Section (1) of Article I;

(b) Thirty Thousand Dollars ($30,000) in money of the United States of America, or its equivalent in money of the Netherlands Government, at the then rate of exchange, for each of the articles called for in sub-division (b) of Section (1) of Article I.

ARTICLE VI

(1) The Contractor will hold and save the Government, its representatives and all other persons acting for it as agent, contractor or otherwise, harmless from all demands or liabilities for alleged use of any patented or unpatented invention, secret process or suggestion in, or in the making or supplying of, the articles or work herein contracted for, and for alleged use of any patented invention in using such articles or work for the purpose for which they are made or supplied, where the demand or liability is based on patents that are owned or controlled by, or under which and to the extent that rights are enjoyed by the Contractor, his officers or employees, or persons in privity with the Contractor; and if and when required, will discharge and secure the Government from all demands or liabilities on account thereof by proper release from the patentees or claimants, but if such release is not practicable, then by bond or otherwise, and to the satisfaction of the Chief of Air Service.

(2) The Government will, without limitation to the time of completion of this contract in other respects, hold and save the Contractor harmless from all demands or liabilities for alleged use of any patented or unpatented invention, secret process or suggestion in, or in the making or supplying the articles or work herein contracted for, and for alleged use of any patented invention in using such articles or work for the purpose for which they are made or supplied, where the demand or liability is based on patents that are not owned or controlled by or under which rights are not enjoyed by the Contractor, his officers or employees or persons in privity with the Contractor; provided, immediate notice of any such demand or liability and of any legal proceedings connected therewith is given in writing by the Contractor to the Contracting Officer; and provided further, that the Government may intervene in any such demand or proceeding and in its discretion may defend the same or make settlement thereof, and the Contractor shall furnish all information in his possession and all assistance of his employees requested by the Government.

(3) The Contractor agrees to grant, and by the execution of this contract does grant to the Government, without further consideration,

the irrevocable but non-exclusive right and license to make, have made, use and sell, for governmental purposes only, any and all parts, machines, manufactures, compositions of matter and/or designs, and to practice or cause to be practiced, any and all discoveries, inventions, improvements, and/or suggestions that may be or may have been made, perfected or devised by the Contractor, his representatives, associates, co-operators, and/or employees in connection with or in pursuance of the performance of this contract, or may be in any manner used in the articles contracted for herein, under any and all patents and other rights based upon such discoveries, inventions, improvements and/or suggestions. Said right and license hereby granted shall extend throughout the United States and its territories, and shall remain in force and effect for the full period of said patents or other rights.

ARTICLE VII

The Contractor agrees to properly care for and be responsible for all Government property delivered to it for installation in the articles contracted for hereunder or for use in connection with the performance of this contract.

ARTICLE VIII

Neither this contract, nor any interest herein, shall be transferred by the Contractor to any other party, except to the extent permitted by Section 3477, United States Revised Statutes.

ARTICLE IX

No Member of or Delegate to Congress, or Resident Commissioner, is or shall be admitted to any share or part of this contract, or to any benefit that may arise therefrom; but this Article shall not apply to this contract so far as it may be within the operation or exceptions of Section 116, of the act of Congress approved March 4, 1909 (35 Stats..1109).

ARTICLE X

The Contractor expressly warrants that he has employed no third person to solicit or obtain this contract in his behalf, or to cause or procure the same to be obtained upon compensation in any way contingent, in whole or in part, upon such procurement; and that he has not paid, or promised or agreed to pay, to any third person, in consideration of such procurement, or in compensation for services in connection therewith, any brokerage, commission, or percentage upon the amount receivable by him hereunder; and that he has not, in estimating the contract price or compensation demanded by him, included any sum by reason of any such brokerage, commission, or percentage; and that all moneys payable to him hereunder are free from obligation to any other person for services rendered or supposed to have been rendered, in the procurement of this contract. The Comtractor further agrees that any breach of this warranty shall constitute adequate cause for the annulment of this contract by the Government, and that the Government may retain to its own use from any sums due or to become due hereunder an amount equal to any brokerage, commission, or percentage so paid or agreed to be paid; provided, however, that this covenant does not apply to the selling of goods through a bona fide commercial representative employed by the Contractor in the regular course of his business in dealing with customers other than the Government and whose compensation is paid, in whole or in part, by commissions on sales made, nor to the selling of goods through established commercial or selling agencies regularly engaged in selling such goods.

ARTICLE XI

The Contractor agrees to furnish to the Contracting Officer, whenever requested so to do, a full statement and report of the progress of the work up to and including the date of such request.

ARTICLE XII

Any question or dispute which may arise under this contract shall be settled by three persons, one of whom shall be appointed by the Contractor, one by the Contracting Officer, and the third by the two persons so appointed and the decision of a majority of these three persons shall be final and binding on both parties.

IN WITNESS WHEREOF, the parties aforesaid have executed this contract in quintuplicate as of the date first hereinbefore written.

Witnesses:

_____   _____
                                             ANTHONY H. G. FOKKER

_____

_____   UNITED STATES OF AMERICA

_____   By _____
                                                R. H. FLEET,
                                                Captain, A. S.,
                                                United States Army,
                                                Contracting Officer.

Considered and Recommended DEC 9 1920
prior to execution by the Government.
...Engineering Division, Air Service

APPROVED DEC 9 1920
By Authority of the Chief of Air Service.
THURMAN H. BANE, Major A. S.
Chief of Engineering Division, Air Service

SPECIFICATION TO APPLY ON CONTRACT NO. 344,
FOR TWO FOKKER TRANSPORT MONOPLANES.

Type: Cantilever Monoplane, F-4.

Engine: 400-H.P. Liberty 12-cylinder.

Planes: 3-ply covered, 4-bolt attachment.

Fuselage: Fokker system, steel tube, fabric covered.

Gasoline
supply: Gravity only, four hours capacity.

Chassis: Special reinforced V type, rubber sprung.

Seating Arrangement: Cabin with removable seats for 8 passengers.

Load: 4 hours fuel plus 2000 lbs.

Approximate dimensions:
    Span   - 62 feet
    Length - 42 feet

Approximate Weight:
    Empty - 5100 lbs.
    Loaded - 8000 lbs.

    The following instruments shall be supplied and installed by Contractor in each airplane:

    One Aneroid (British Standard Type)
    One Air Speed Indicator (British Standard Type)
    One Radiator Thermometer (British Standard Type)
    All switches necessary
    One Gasoline Level Gauge
    All Pressure Gauges (if required)

    The following equipment shall be furnished by the Government, and shall be installed by the Contractor in one of the two airplanes of this type, and so returned to the Government with that airplane when delivered:

    One 400-H.P. Liberty 12-cylinder engine
    One Propeller, of suitable design
    One Tachometer
    One six-foot Tachometer Shaft, complete.

    One of the two airplanes shall be delivered complete with engine, propeller and all instruments and accessories installed therein. The other shall be delivered complete except for engine, propeller, tachometer and tachometer shaft. This airplane shall in all other respects be an exact duplicate of the airplane delivered with the engine, propeller, tachometer and tachometer shaft installed therein.

Dayton, Ohio, U. S. A.

December 4, 1920.

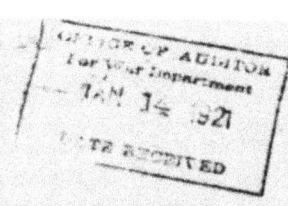

CERTIFICATE OF CONTRACTING OFFICER
In connection with contract 544,
with Anthony H. G. Fokker.

    I certify that I am the duly authorized Contracting Officer of and for the Engineering Division, Air Service; that on December 2, 1920, on behalf of the Government, I entered into Engineering Division contract 544 with Anthony H. G. Fokker, an individual, of Amsterdam, Holland, said contract requiring the Contractor to design, manufacture and assemble for, and deliver to the Government, two Fokker single-seater armored combat monoplanes for Eighteen Thousand ($18,000.00) Dollars each, and two Fokker transport monoplanes, for Thirty Thousand ($30,000.00) Dollars each; that said contract was entered into without advertising or competitive bidding, for the reason that the above-named Contractor is the designer and sole manufacturer of said types of airplanes, and competition is therefore impracticable; that I have investigated the price charged, and consider the same a reasonable price for said articles; that said contract, before execution by the Government, was submitted to the Advisory Purchase Board of said Engineering Division, for consideration and recommendation, and said Board recommended execution of the same; that said project was directed, and said contract approved by the Chief of said Engineering Division, Air Service; and further, in compliance with the provisions of paragraph 517, Army Regulations, special authority for this purchase was obtained from the Secretary of War, under date of December 30, 1920.

Dated Jan. 10, 1921.

R. H. FLEET, Captain, A. S.,
Contracting Officer,
Engineering Division,
Air Service.

```
                    AIR SERVICE
                 ENGINEERING DIVISION
                    McCOOK FIELD

Contract Section
                                         DAYTON, OHIO Jan. 14, 1921

    From:      The Contracting Officer

    To:        Auditor for the War Department, Washington, D. C.

    Subject:   Contract 544.

         1. Herewith find one original of a certificate, which
    you are requested to attach to the copy of the above contract
    now in your possession.

                                          R. H. FLEET,
                                          Captain, A. S.
```

Anthony Fokker as Aircraft Designer

[The following passages are reproduced from *The Aeroplane, An Historical Survey*, by Charles Gibbs-Smith (London, 1960, pp. 271-272, 335-336) with kind permission of the author.]

One of the most curious and interesting questions of aviation history related to the reputation of the famous Dutchman Fokker, whose name was borne by many outstanding aircraft. Fokker's reputation as a designer has recently been questioned by Mr. A. R. Weyl, A.F.R. Ae. S. Mr. Weyl has kindly sent me the information which follows:

The name of Fokker is connected with many engineering achievements in aviation. Fokker aeroplanes and their constructional features have widely influenced the development of aeronautics.

The late A. H. G. Fokker was indeed a most remarkable personality. Yet his merits about the design and the development of the aircraft which bear his name, are more than doubtful. He was a most accomplished test pilot of great skill and much courage. His fine sense for the handling qualities of aeroplanes, and his eagerness to try modifications in flight much contributed to the success of his aircraft. There, too, cannot be any doubt that he has influenced the development by determining the policy to be followed for the evolution of new aircraft types.

Research shows, however, that claims raised by Fokker in his autobiography (Fokker and Gould, *The Flying Dutchman*) are not in agreement with verifiable facts, and that the legend of Fokker having designed his own aeroplanes cannot be upheld.

A. H. G. Fokker actually never designed an aircraft (or a weapon) on his own; he had, in fact, no technical gift to do so. At best, he inspired his various designers on the basis of his excellent information on developments in the aeronautical industry. In the few instances in which he seems to have done more, by compelling his designers to adopt constructional schemes of his own, dismal failures were the result.

Fokker was most eager to be appreciated as an engineering expert and as the actual designer of his aeroplanes. His eagerness led him to the childish practice of 'sealing off' the designers employed by him against any contacts outside the firm or with the aeronautical authorities. They were not allowed to attend design conferences with the customers (the German Army authorities), or to be present when the official type tests or strength experimentation on new Fokker aircraft were conducted. They also had withheld from them all the official technical information or documentation which ought to have reached them. Besides, Fokker never engaged qualified design engineers; his pretext was that they were "not practical enough."

The original Fokker "Spiders" of 1911 to 1913 were designed by Jacob Goedecker, an eminent aeronautical engineer of high qualifications at Mainz. Goedecker's work, too, supplied all these aircraft ready for assembly in Fokker's workshops at Johannisthal till 1913. By then, Fokker had established a workshop of his own which was soon transferred to Schwerin. Among the few skilled craftsmen in this workshop was a welder, Reinhold Platz. He later became the unaided designer of the historic Fokker fighters (the Fok. Dr.I triplane; the Fok. D.VII biplane; and the Fok. D.VIII 'Flying Razor' parasol monoplane) and of the famous Fokker transport monoplanes between 1919 and 1934. Platz, too, had his hand in the development of the famous Fokker fighters of 1915 which were basic modifications of the French Morane-Saulnier design.

His predecessor Martin Kreutzer fatally crashed in July 1916 whilst flight-testing a production fighter biplane (Fok. D.I). Fokker's star as an aircraft manufacturer was then nearly extinct. The Army authorities found fault with the performance of his aeroplanes and with their structual reliability; he was compelled to produce training aircraft of the AEG design. Fokker engaged two new designers in quick succession to improve his position as a designing manufacturer; none achieved a new prototype. Platz, by then in charge of an experimental department for structural development, suggested to Fokker to let him have a try at the design of a new aircraft. Within a few weeks, a revolutionary biplane with completely cantilever wings and radically new controls was accomplished. From then on, Fokker fighters reached the top of the German air development.

Platz was ill-equipped as a designer. He had served an apprenticeship but had no engineering training. The rudiments of statics and aerodynamics were alien to him. So he had to create his own methods for the design of progressive aeroplanes. His stressing methods (based upon systematic structural experimentation) were, after a year, so reliable and so accurate that he was in a position to correct calculations made by the structural experts of the German Research Establishment for Aeronautics (shortly after the war).

During World War I, the German air authorities never learned who actually designed the famous Fokker aeroplanes. Their engineering experts at Adlershof were puzzled how this young Dutchman was able to achieve such excellent fighter aeroplanes whilst he was unable to answer their simplest technical questions on these aircraft. Fokker's answers were invariably flippant or impudent. The experts were, however, naive enough to believe that Fokker invented his aircraft. They, too, never suspected that the actual designer was even denied the official handbook which set out the technical requirements of the Army for their aeroplanes.

R. Platz had his most fruitful period of creating new aircraft types when Fokker fled from Germany on account of income-tax frauds soon after the Armistice (in his autobiography, he blamed the 'bloodthirsty revolutionary' workers of his factory; in fact, it was the tax inspector armed by the public prosecutor!)

R. Platz, a man of amazing engineering capacity, is now living near Hamburg as a refugee from the Russian-dominated zone of Germany; he is completely forgotten in the world of aeronautical engineering. Apart from Fokker's hypocritical autobiography, Platz' surfeit of modesty has contributed to this.

My forthcoming work endeavours to bring to light the facts behind the Fokker-aeroplane development from the official documents of the German Army Flying Corps and from evidence by R. Platz and by other witnesses of the period concerned. . . .

With the kind permission of Mr. J. van Hattum, I reprint here a letter he wrote to the magazine *Aero Modeller* (December 1957):

"Dear Sir,

"In your issue for September of this year, Mr. P. L. Gray asserts that he has been supplied with material which would show that the Fokker D.VII single-seat fighter was not designed by Anthony Fokker but by his designer, Reinhold Platz. The same would apply to other Fokker aircraft.

"If this is true, then it would be nothing unusual for an aircraft constructor to be assisted in larger or smaller measure by a technical team, headed by his chief designer. Fokker, with much of his time taken up by many of the business affairs a manufacturer has to attend to, though he later delegated much to others could not be expected to stand a full working day behind one of his firm's drawing boards. This is true of all aircraft constructors, who may have been Jacks of all trades at the start of their careers, but who had to call in technical assistance when their business grew.

"Fokker, too, had a technical staff, headed first by Herr Palm and later by Herr Marton Kreutzer, killed in 1916 on the D.I Fighter he designed himself. When Fokker adopted welding for the steel parts of one of his early aircraft, the Spider, other constructors had already used this new technique in aircraft engineering. Mr. Platz however, was an expert in welding and could be regarded as an authority on the subject. He moved with Fokker from Johannisthal to Schwerin in the autumn of 1913, which proves Fokker's genius in spotting talent and making good use of it. It should be pointed out that in those days the title of chief designer did not exist in the Fokker works; he was simply known as the designer.

"Fokker has never asserted that he himself entirely designed or worked out the aircraft his works made. But he did indicate the general line and layout of most of his products. And when we use the word "his," it is applied in the same sense as it would be to Sir Henry Royce's cars, or to Count Zeppelin's airships or, to Geoffrey de Havilland. They all put their personal stamp on their products as head of a team.

"However, building aircraft to a design is not all the story. In many cases aircraft designed in the Fokker drawing office had too short a fuselage, i.e., too small a tail moment-arm. Fokker, as a first-class pilot, could feel the defects before they could do harm, and had alterations made. He was never really satisfied with an aircraft; in his book Flying Dutchman, he writes: "No one has yet found as many flaws in an airplane of mine as I could find myself."

"Aircraft should not only be built, they should also have good flying qualities. Fokker was the ideal test-pilot, who flew by feel and if he had not taken charge of this second phase, that of testing and altering until the plane was to his satisfaction, a job which he did all by himself until the beginning of the 'twenties, not so much would have come of the world-famous name. It was Fokker himself who was responsible for the nonstalling properties of his aircraft and which made them so safe and well-liked.

"There is no doubt that Fokker and his designer mutually inspired each other, and the result is well-known. To unravel the past in order to find out just how much was contributed by the one and how much by the other, would be almost impossible at this stage, and, it seems to me, rather unfair to Fokker who is not here to give his views on the matter. Though it may sound crude, we would like to put the question whether his designers would have achieved as much without his leadership and guidance and whether Fokker would not have achieved the same with other collaborators, and the aircraft would still have borne his personal stamp.

"To come out now with the discovery that Fokker did not completely design his aircraft himself, is about as sound as to suggest that a writer did not really create his work because he had research workers collecting and sifting data for him."

(Signed) J. van Hattum

Royal Netherlands Aero Club
The Hague, Holland

Log of DH–4B Accompanying Second Flight Attempt

Special plane 63780, a DH–4B, with Lt. G. L. Weber as pilot and Lt. J. P. Richter as observer, accompanied the second attempt of the Army Air Service Transport T–2 on its Transcontinental Flight from Rockwell Field, Calif., Nov. 3, 1922. Its log follows:

Log of DH–4B

6:10 a.m.	Left Rockwell. Circle to (the) T–2, 400 ft over north end of island, both planes. Circle island and leave starting point 6:18 a.m. Altitude 500 ft to 600. Mission Bay 6:24—T–2 1000 ft.
6:30	Opposite Torrey Pines. T–2 about 1600 ft. We have to rev. 1300–1350 to stay behind.
6:37	Hodges Dam. 1700 ft. T–2 about 2000 ft.
6:43	Cross R.R. and Highway to Escondido. T–2 about 2400 ft alt and way off to our right.
6:56	Temecula 2100 T–2 following off to right and behind about 2600–2800. Nice and clear in valley.
7:05	T–2 bears off to left we continue toward Beaumont.
7:11	T–2 turns to take up course with us and loses about 200–250 ft alt. T–2 also lost some alt. after passing Temecula.
7:18	T–2 crosses east of Hemet north of San Jacinto about one in. to spare.
7:24	Arrive Southern Pacific (R.R.) south of Beaumont 2800 ft.
7:25	Banking about 2700 ft. T–2 traveling much faster we have to rev. 14–1500 air speed goes up to 90–105 with tail wind. Struck some rough air.
7:30	We drop down to 2000 ft. T–2 stays about 2400.
7:35	Very heavy head winds and bumps. Probably feel it so bad because we are only rev. 1300–1350.
7:40	Hugo. Alt. 1600 T–2 about 2000. Air is smooth again and on tail.
7:46	Palm Springs. 1200 ft. Our generator is on fritz. Start running on one switch, the right.
8:00	Salton, alt 1000. T–2 several hundred feet above us.

Log of DH-4B—Continued

8:10............... Motor working badly. Change to left switch O.K.
8:20............... Niland alt 1900 T-2 behind and above.
8:33............... T-2 passed from sight off to our left over the Chocolate Mountains, alt above 2000.
8:44............... T-2 back in sight.
8:50............... Yuma to our right and south, we start to tell T-2 goodbye.
8:52............... Left them about 20 miles north of Yuma, alt 2000. Visibility very good. Air a little rough. They were headed east towards Chimney Peak—we started home.
9:00............... Cross S.P. near Cactus 2500 ft. Very cold.
9:19............... El Centro 4000 ft.
9:50............... Carrizo Gorge 6600 ft.
10:19.............. El Cajon 3000 ft.
10:23.............. La Mesa.
10:25.............. San Diego.
10:28.............. Land Rockwell Field.

Picture Credits

Unless otherwise indicated, numbers identify photo negatives of the National Air Museum, Smithsonian Institution.

Front.	National Archives	22	A51414
1	U.S. Air Service 10561	23	A53907
2	U.S. Air Service 10677	24	A31967E, Fokker Netherlands
3	U.S. Air Service 17822	25	Frank Dobias (sketch)
4	A45881	26	A48248, Fokker Netherlands
5	A49911	27	A47481, Fokker Netherlands
6	No copies available	28	A47482, Fokker Netherlands
7	A45798F, Col. Kelly	29	A45288B, U.S. Air Service
8	A46536, Col. Kelly	30	A48241B
9	A46536B, Col. Kelly	31	A45800E, Reinhold Platz
10	A46536C, Col. Kelly	32	A43639L, Fokker Netherlands
11	Smithsonian A45865, Col. Kelly	33	A48643A
12	A48089, U.S. Air Service	34	A47507
13	A48067D, Reinhold Platz	35	A47483, Fokker Netherlands
14	A48067A, Reinhold Platz	36	A47506
15	A48067E, Reinhold Platz	37	A47506A
16	A48067B, Reinhold Platz	38	A47478
17	A52749	39	A48744
18	A48530, Fokker Netherlands	40	A48643
19	AP6369A	41	U.S. Air Service 163149
20	P63282	42	U.S. Air Service 10917
21	A52556	43	A45860

Bibliography

FOKKER, ANTHONY H. G., and GOULD, BRUCE. *Flying Dutchman*. New York: Henry Holt, 1931.

Fokker V-45 (F-II). *Aeroplane* (March 31, 1920), vol. 18, no. 13, p. 680.

Fokker F-III. *Flight* (May 26, 1921), vol. 13, no. 21, p. 355.

Fokker F-IV. *Flight* (December 29, 1921), vol. 13, no. 52, p. 858.

GIBBS-SMITH, CHARLES H. *The Aeroplane, An Historical Survey*. London: Her Majesty's Stationery Office, 1960.

MACREADY, JOHN A. Nonstop Flight Across America, *National Geographic Magazine* (July 1924), vol. 46, no. 1, pp. 1–83.

Standard Oil Bulletin (September 1923), vol. 11, no. 5, p. 13.

The following reports may be found at the Air Force Museum Library:

War Department, *Air Service Report D 52.1/1*. Preparation of T-2 for Nonstop Transcontinental Flight.

War Department, *Air Service Report D 52.1/3*.

War Department, *Air Service Report 2146*. Engineering Features of the T-2.

War Department, *Air Service Report 2068*. Report of Nonstop Flight.

Continuation of War Department, *Air Service Report 2068*, Nov. 20, 1922.

The following material is now filed in the National Air Museum Library:

Air Service Information Circular, vol. 4, no. 377. Technical Orders, no. 27, July, 1922.

Air Service Information Circular, vol. 4, no. 378. Technical Orders, no. 28, Sept., 1922.

Air Service Information Circular, vol. 4, no. 391. Technical Supplement. *Report of European Trip* by Gen. Mitchell, 1st Lt. Clayton Bissell, Aero Engr. Alfred Verville, Nov. 1, 1922.

Air Service Technical Information Circular, vol. 5, no. 426. Technical Bulletin 33, March 1923.

Air Service Technical Information Circular, vol. 5, no. 427. Technical Bulletin 34, May and June 1923.

www.ingramcontent.com/pod-product-compliance
Lightning Source LLC
Chambersburg PA
CBHW080522110426
42742CB00017B/3199